BOLOGNA

...on foot

The Trademark TAITA PRESS belongs to: Ediservizi s.r.l.

Coordinator : **Pino Cantafio**
Art Director: **Michele Accursi**
Text : **freely inspired by Wikipedia**
Historical researches : **Fulvio Cantafio**
Photographs : **Ediservizi s.r.l.**
Printed in the month of May 2011
By : **GRAFICHE GARATTONI srl – Viserba di Rimini (RN)**
On behalf of :
EDISERVIZI s.r.l.
Via Zanardi 106/6
40131 Bologna
info@taitapress.com
www.taitapress.com

Note: the Publisher and Editor have carefully checked the information herein. However, we assume absolutely no responsibility for any inaccuracies contained in the text. Besides, we thank you in advance for any remarks and/or suggestions you may wish to send us.

SUMMARY

FOREWORD

Dear reader,

Welcome to Bologna and thanks for choosing our guide.

Bologna is a medieval city, so it was surrounded by walls, to fortify it against invasions, and by access doors to the city with drawbridges.

The walls do not exist any more, except for some ruins, while the doors remain to preside over today's Bologna, most of which in good state of preservation having recently undergone a significant renovation.

Our intention with this guide is to establish tours that can enable you to visit the important city's buildings, and to supply historical notes about them and information on their architecture and any works housed inside, as well as useful information to better benefit from the city.

This guide has been divided for the visitor into 4 tours inside the walls and one tour outside the walls, that you are recommended to make by bus or by your own vehicle.

The tours inside the walls start from Piazza Maggiore, Bologna's heart.

The tour outside the walls starts from Porta Mascarella.

For the sake of convenience, the indications on the tours are highlighted with green.

The Editor

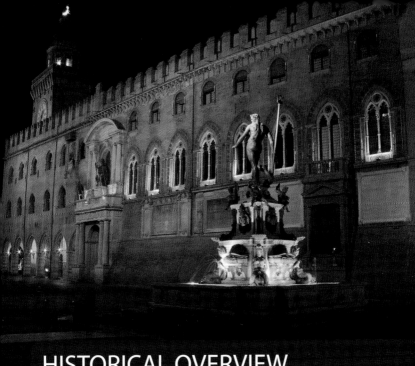

HISTORICAL OVERVIEW

The first traces indicating the presence of human beings on the Bologna's territory date back to approximately 5000 years before the Christ's birth. This is the Neolithic Age, and the presence of small villages and hovels, together with wooden tools, bone and polish stone, clearly suggest that there were geographically stable populations dedicated to farming and breeding.

Only from the 18th century BC bronze started to replace stone for tools daily used by the populations of that age.

Toward the 9th century BC (First Iron Age) the Villanoviana culture developed inside the territory (this culture takes the name after a small town in the Bologna's hinterland - Villanova -, where in 1853 a group of sepulchres full of tools and other accessories dating back to that historical period was discovered). The characterizing elements were the progressive use of iron for several manufactured products, the development of the techniques employed to better work bronze, the proved use of cremation of the dead, all features also found in the early Etruscan people.

Toward the 6th century BC, Felsinea (Bologna's name at that time) became a flourishing built-up area, and assumed the role of reference centre in Po valley. The merits of the Etruscan influence were the cultural enrichment and the predisposition of the local populations to being open about the world outside.

Toward the 4th century BC, Po valley was invaded by the Celtic populations that Romans called Gauls.

The tribe that occupied Felsinea (or Felsina?) was the Galli Boi tribe. They did not have an urban culture and preferred to settle on the territory in a scattered manner, near woods and farmable soils, thus causing the existing Etruscan built-up area to decay.

In 189 BC the Romans occupied the territory and forced the Galli Boi tribe to move towards the most uncomfortable areas in the Po valley (woods and wetland areas), thus creating the Latin colony of Bononia.

In the colonised territory about 400 sq km were divided into squares of 700 m per side approximately, that were assigned to a great number of settlers, while one square was assigned to the city of Bononia thus allowing it to develop.

In 88 BC the Bononia's inhabitants finally obtained the Roman citizenship, with all the consequent burdens and honours.

During the time the city became a Municipium and was provided with paved streets, a sewage system, thermae, public buildings (among which a great theatre), and an aqueduct that drew water from Setta river and, after a course of about 20 Km, distributed it to the city.

At the beginning of the 4th century AD, following the last persecution of Christians ordered by Diocletian, Bologna has its first martyrs, Vitalis and Agricola, whose relics were buried in 392 by Saint Ambrose in the spot where once a pagan building stood (original element of the future Abbazia di S. Stefano).

After Diocletian died, the Emperor Constantine succeeded him. He allowed the Bologna's citizens to have their first Bishop: Zamo.

In the 5th century AD Saint Petronius was Bishop of Bologna (he was the eighth Bishop of the city and its future patron saint), and after he died his body was buried in the Basilica di S. Stefano.

Following the collapse of the Western Roman Empire, Bologna suffered continuous invasions of Germanic populations, even struggling against each other, until the war between Ostrogoths and Byzantines broke out, devastating Italy for more than twenty years.

After a short peaceful period, the Longobards invaded northern Italy and only found an insurmountable barrier near the Byzantine Exarchate of Ravenna; thus Bologna became the closest city to the new invaders, and was able to effectively defend itself only because it was surrounded by a circle of walls made of selenite (large blocks of raw gypsum).

In 727 the Longobard king Liutprand conquered the city and reigned over it until 774, when the city was freed by Charles the Great. He handed it over to the Pope, who had it governed by a duke until the end of the 9th century.

In 896 (during the age of the city-states) Bologna became part of the Italic Reign, and a count ruled the city (sometimes through assignment, at other times by heritage) until the beginning of the 12th century.

Between the 11th and the 12th centuries the "Studio", the prodrome of the oldest university in Europe, was founded. The lectures held by Irnerio and Pepone, masters of Roman law, attracted young people from all over the Europe, whose economical contribution allowed the "Studio Bolognese" to be supported.

At the beginning of the 12th century Bologna also became a free city-state.

At that time the Bologna's noble families built a large quantity of towers, both for prestige sake and defence, since conflicts, even violent ones, often occurred due to the exercise of the power.

Moreover, following the economic revival, the network of navigable channels with which the territory was provided since the Roman epoch, was enlarged in that period by realizing in the city the Reno and Savena channels, that were added to the Aposa stream and the Navile channel, thus allowing a manufacturing and commercial economy to develop.

The economic and demographic development occurred in that period was a positive consequence of the Peace of Constance of 1183 signed between Frederick Barbarossa and the city-states of the first Lombard League, to which Bologna also belonged, and obviously allowed the dimension of the city's territory to increase, thus causing it to be surrounded by a second circle of walls, called "Mura dei Torresotti", for safety's sake.

In that period the today's Piazza Maggiore and the Palazzo Comunale were also realized, while the city centre was urbanely remodelled by demolishing a whole district of tenement blocks developed in a disorderly manner.

Moreover, some of the towns of the current hinterland began to be born thanks to the economic development, which occasioned an increase in labour demand and attracted people even from far away lands.

In 1249, the Bologna's citizens defeated Emperor Frederick II at Fossalta, after years of battles between the second Lombard League and the imperial armies. They captured King Enzo (son of the Emperor) and forced him to a golden confinement in the city (in the today's Palazzo Re Enzo), where he stayed until his death in 1272.

During this century, in 1256, a law was also issued enfranchising the serfs from their total dependence from the feudal lord, thus making them free men: the Legge del Paradiso (Paradise Law).

Compared to the previous one, the 14th century was characterized by economic decline due to unpopular governments following one another and military setbacks.

The Bologna's plebs, compelled by the consequences of the economic crisis, rebelled in 1334, and destroyed the Rocca of the Porta Galliera, one of the most important doors as for the "toll".

Unfortunately, it was destroyed several times also during the 15th and 16th centuries.

In 1390 the erection of the Basilica dedicated to Saint Petronius, who later became the city's patron saint, was started as thanks for the independence recovered by the city-state in 1376, after suffering the rule of the Seigniory of the Visconti family, who acquired the city following the depopulation occasioned by the Black Death and also after the papal dominion.

In the early 15th century Giovanni Bentivoglio succeeded in being elected "perpetual Gonfaloniere", so the fortune of the Bentivoglio family began. Actually they ruled the city for about a century.

When the King of France Charles VIII came to Italy (to support the Pontifical State), the stability between the Italian states and Bologna broke down; after the flight of Giovanni II (the last Bentivoglio), on June 13th 1512 Bologna submitted to Papa Julius II and became the "northern capital" of the Pontifical State.

The submission arrangements envisaged that city's government would be entrusted to two authorities, namely the Pontifical Legate and the Senate (appointed by the nobles), whose decisions had to be mutually agreed.

On February 24th 1530, Pope Clement VII crowned emperor Charles V in the Basilica di San Petronio. The splendour of the celebrations organized for this occasion did not succeed in removing from the city's memory the acts of violence and robberies committed by both the papal army and the imperial army during the few months in which they stayed in Bologna.

In the 16th century the seat for all the lectures of the "Studio Bolognese", that had gained unbounded prestige, became the Archiginnasio, according to the will of the Papal Legate who intended to better control the education given there.

In that same period Piazza Maggiore was also completed, thus assuming the current appearance thanks to the construction of the Fontana del Nettuno and the Palazzo dei Banchi. Instead, the Basilica di San Petronio remained unfinished.

At the beginning of the 17th century, Bologna experienced another period of economic and demographic contraction as a consequence of a new plague epidemic and years of famine.

The agriculture and the small manufacturing industry still surviving (silk and hemp) did not enable the lower class to enjoy acceptable conditions of life, so the poverty spread.

The 18th century is characterized by the response the city was able to give to an increased cultural demand. Actually the Archiginnasio, flagship of the "Studio Bolognese" of the origin, was found to have obsolete teaching methods for the exigencies of that epoch, thus the Istituto delle Scienze (Institute of Science) was founded. It was provided with chemistry, physics and natural science laboratories, and even a specola for the astronomers; the prime mover of this philanthropic initiative was Luigi Ferdinando Marsili.

In that same period the Teatro Comunale, designed by Bibiena (Antonio Galli) and featuring an impeccable acoustic, was inaugurated.

On June 19th 1796 Napoleon's troops entered Bologna, thus putting an end of the "Senate – Legate" government that had been ruling the city for some centuries. Bologna became part of the Cisalpina Republic (later called Italic Reign).

The Napoleon's edicts changed the city's life, convents and churches were expropriated and handed over to the State, or they were sold to private individuals; ancient guilds of arts and crafts were suppressed, and new theatres were founded.

In 1815 the Council of Vienna handed the city back to the Pope.

In 1831 the city attempted to rebel, the Papal Legate was forced away and the Pope's temporal power over Bologna was stated to be decayed. But later the Austrian army, called by the Pope, succeeded in stopping any ambition and handed the city back to the Pontifical State.

In 1848 (August 8th) the Bologna's citizens managed to drive the Austrians out of the city, but after few months (May 1849) the Austrians occupied it again and remained there until June 12th 1859, where the Pope's temporal power over the city ceased.

In 1861, after the second world of independence, the city became part of the Kingdom of Italy.

In the early 20th century an impressive city plan enlarged the city's main road axes, planning the demolition of the walls and so creating the conditions for the city's growth and development.

In that period, the first experience in Italy of gas and water services supplied by municipality was started. Moreover, there were a significant revitalization of industry and the creation of a wide cooperative movement.

After being ruled by socialist forces, in 1920 the city, following the rise of fascism, began to be governed by Heads (Podestà) appointed by the regime.

The Second World War, the front of which was only 20 Km away from the city during the last phase of the conflict, brought vast destructions.

This nightmare came to an end on April 21st 1945, the Liberation day. The Bologna's citizens drove the German occupants out as a reaction against the massacre of civil populations occurred in Marzabotto.

During the spring of 1945, Giuseppe Dozza was appointed Mayor of Bologna, and he was always reappointed for about 20 years thanks to the citizens' appreciation for his works.

The commitment lavished by the citizens and the social and economic forces enabled the city to rapidly recover and reach a good level of socio-economic well-being; this was the merit of the traditional industriousness of Bologna's citizens.

Today the city embodies a great economic reality of the nation. However it is not only this, actually Bologna features an important railway station and a fundamental motorway junction, both crucial national crossing points. All these elements, together with entrepreneurial ability, efficiency of services and appreciation of the "good life", allow the city to be in the first places in Italy as for quality of life is concerned.

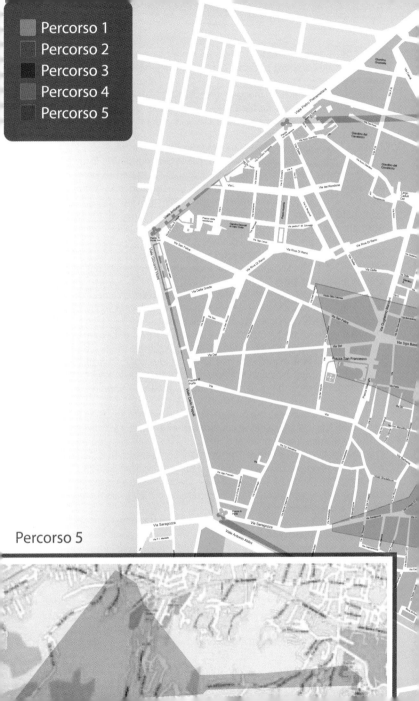

TOUR

1

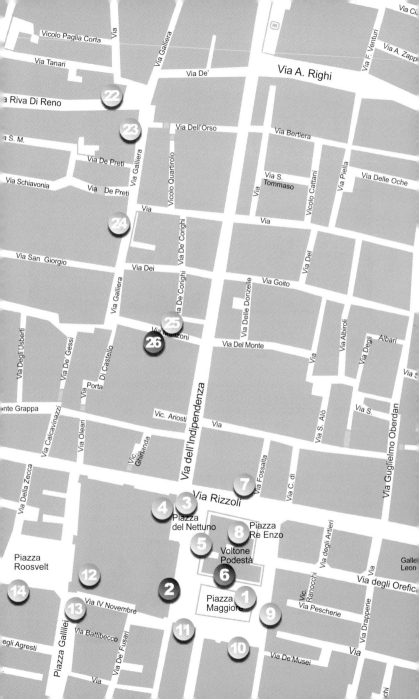

PIAZZA MAGGIORE

🚏 **Piazza Maggiore** 🚌 line n. 11, 13, 14, 17, 18, 19, 20, 25, 27, 29, 30 (Rizzoli) A (P.Maggiore) B, BLQ Aerobus (S.Pietro)

UTILITY

This is the main square of Bologna, surrounded by buildings of historical importance. On one side it is bounded by the already mentioned Palazzo Comunale, which skirts the Piazza del Nettuno at whose centre stands the fountain with the statue by Giambologna. On another side it is bounded by the Basilica di San Petronio, with its peculiar façade. On the other sides there is the Palazzo Re Enzo and the Palazzo dei Banchi with its beautiful portico.

The area of Piazza Maggiore developed in the 13th century, when it was surrounded by popular buildings that the Municipality acquired to knock them down. However, only in the 15th century the square assumed the current appearance, while in the 16th century, at Pope's request through the Cardinal Legate Carlo Borromeo, the whole area was renovated with the construction of the adjacent Piazza Nettuno, already mentioned.

In 1860 the square was named after Victor Emmanuel II, but in 1945 the statue of the sovereign was moved to the Giardini Margherita, where it still stands, and the square was called Piazza Maggiore.

It represents one of the most important squares in Italy, and measures 115 metres in length and 60 metres in width. At those times it was the venue for the market, tournaments and popular feasts. Today it represents a meeting point for Bologna's citizens and is also used for election meetings, public demonstrations and spectacles.

Put your back to the Basilica di San Petronio and the palace you will see on your left is:

BI-09
MP3

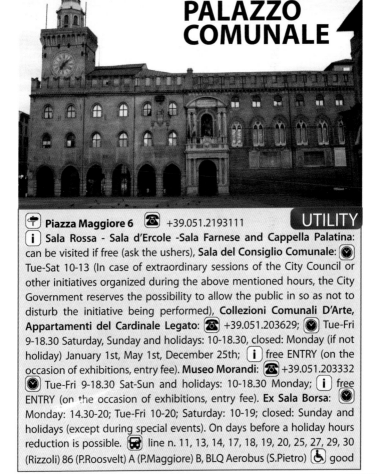

PALAZZO COMUNALE

UTILITY

Piazza Maggiore 6 ☎ +39.051.2193111

ⓘ **Sala Rossa - Sala d'Ercole -Sala Farnese and Cappella Palatina:** can be visited if free (ask the ushers), **Sala del Consiglio Comunale:** 🕐 Tue-Sat 10-13 (In case of extraordinary sessions of the City Council or other initiatives organized during the above mentioned hours, the City Government reserves the possibility to allow the public in so as not to disturb the initiative being performed), **Collezioni Comunali D'Arte, Appartamenti del Cardinale Legato:** ☎ +39.051.203629; 🕐 Tue-Fri 9-18.30 Saturday, Sunday and holidays: 10-18.30, closed: Monday (if not holiday) January 1st, May 1st, December 25th; ⓘ free ENTRY (on the occasion of exhibitions, entry fee). **Museo Morandi:** ☎ +39.051.203332 🕐 Tue-Fri 9-18.30 Sat-Sun and holidays: 10-18.30 Monday; ⓘ free ENTRY (on the occasion of exhibitions, entry fee). **Ex Sala Borsa:** 🕐 Monday: 14.30-20; Tue-Fri 10-20; Saturday: 10-19; closed: Sunday and holidays (except during special events). On days before a holiday hours reduction is possible. 🚌 line n. 11, 13, 14, 17, 18, 19, 20, 25, 27, 29, 30 (Rizzoli) 86 (P.Roosvelt) A (P.Maggiore) B, BLQ Aerobus (S.Pietro) ♿ good

The first palace was a complex whose origin dates back to the 14th century. It was commissioned by Francesco Accursio, jurist and master of law in the Studio Bolognese, that used it as his dwelling. It underwent many enlargements and transformations, and it was also used as a city barn for famine times. In 1336 it became the residence of the Elders, the maximum city's magistracy, and thus the seat of the city's government. The *Tower* dates back to 1444.

It was renovated in the 15th century by Fioravante Fioravanti who added the clock of the Torre d'Accursio, which today makes the palace façade striking. Other renovations date back to the 16th century, after the fall of the Bentivoglio family.

Currently the Palace is the seat of the Municipality, and its interior preserves memories of historical and political events of the city.

Access to first floor was also possible through a *cordonata*, designed in the 15th century. This is a slanted flight of low and long steps, which enabled access to the upper floors to litters and men on horseback as well.

On the first floor, the current *Sala del Consiglio Comunale* was frescoed by Angelo Michele Colonna and Gioacchino Pizzoli in the 17th century.

On the second floor there is the *Sala Regia (then Sala Farnese)*, that was the antechamber for every ceremonial. The decorations commemorate

events from the Middle Age to the 17th century. This same hall contains the *Cappella del Legato,* frescoed by Prospero Fontana, where in 1530 emperor Charles V was crowned.

In the halls of the top floor 214 artworks by "Giorgio Morandi", one of the great Masters of the 20th century, are displayed.

The section overlooking the Piazza Nettuno is the seat of the Biblioteca Sala Borsa from 2001.

Above the main door to the palace the statue of Gregory XIII (end of 16th century) sits. It must be recalled that the Bologna's Pope Gregory XIII has the merit to have promoted the Calendar Reform in the second half of the 16th century, thus called "Gregorian Calendar", which nowadays is used all over the world. In that same epoch Father Egnazio Danti also lived in Bologna. He was a prominent mathematician, who joined in the commission for the Calendar Reform.

The Napoleon's troops, that occupied the city at the end of the 19th century, tried to eliminate the symbols of the papal authority from the palace. The statue of Gregory XIII managed to be saved because the figure was transformed from Pope into Bishop: a Mitre was placed on its head instead of the Tiara, while the papal pastoral (ending with a cross) was transformed into an Episcopal pastoral (by replacing the cross by a curl).

Under the large window you see near the statue of God Neptune, two marble eagles can be admired: the one on the left is traditionally attributed to Michelangelo.

Looking downwards and slightly to the left, you will see on the wall the Bologna's ancient measures (foot, arm, pole, measure of roof tile and brick), that were especially useful in that place since the square was the venue of an important medieval market.

FONTANA DEL NETTUNO

🪧 **Piazza del Nettuno - Piazza Re Enzo**

UTILITY

🚌 line n. 11, 13, 14, 17, 18, 19, 20, 25, 27, 29, 30 (Rizzoli) 86 (P.Roosvelt) A (P.Maggiore) B, BLQ Aerobus (S.Pietro)

This is a monumental fountain whose statue was wanted by Pope Pius IV dè Medici (his family was not related to the Florence's Medici, but it had Lombard origins), promoted by the Cardinal Legate of Bologna Carlo Borromeo, and managed by the deputy Legate Pier Donato Cesi

It was designed by the architect and painter Tommaso Laureti in 1563, and was surmounted by the bronze imposing statue representing the God Neptune by the Flemish Mannerist sculptor *Jean de Boulogne da Douai*, called Giambologna. It measures 3.20 m in height and weighs 22 quintals. Due to its dimensions the Bologna's citizens name it "The Giant". It is considered one of the city's symbols.

A CURIOUS NOTE

To build the fountain (completed in 1565) a whole city block was pulled down, while the expenses were divided into the adjacent houses and shops. Giambologna is told to have had the intention to realize the God Neptune with larger genitals, but the papal authority forbade him to. However, the sculptor did not give up, and designed the statue in a manner that from a particular angle the thumb of the Neptune's stretched left hand seems to directly emerge from the lower abdomen, similar to an erect penis. At that time the Bologna's women became upset when looking at the statue of God Neptune, so the papal authority decided to put bronze trousers on it. Actually, the whole fountain has strong erotic value, see for example the nymphs situated on the border spraying water from the breasts.

The gentle steps on your left lead to the

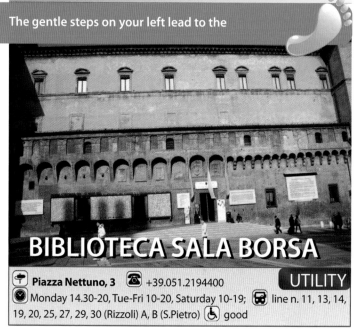

BIBLIOTECA SALA BORSA

Piazza Nettuno, 3 ☎ +39.051.2194400   **UTILITY**
🕐 Monday 14.30-20, Tue-Fri 10-20, Saturday 10-19; 🚌 line n. 11, 13, 14, 19, 20, 25, 27, 29, 30 (Rizzoli) A, B (S.Pietro) ♿ good

It is housed in the Palazzo d'Accursio.

The current hall was inaugurated in 2001.

Under the transparent floor of the current covered square you can admire archaeological finds occasioned by the sedimentation of several civilizations, including the Villanovan civilization dating back to the 7th century, the Felsina's Etruscan one and the Bononia's Roman one.

Over the centuries many transformations took place until the 13th century, when some houses were built above the Roman ruins, among which there was the house of the Bologna's well-known jurist Francesco Accursio.

In 1880 this part of the palace was used as the central point of city's economic and social life, a new building dedicated to stock exchange and stock market operations was erected. The inauguration of the new Sala Borsa occurred on July 17th 1926. During the post-war period it was transformed into a modern indoor stadium, and it was only in 1999 when it was decided to turn the covered square into a library.Today the Sala Borsa is a *multimedia library for general information* aiming at illustrating the contemporaneous culture through different types of documents: books, newpapers, magazines, maps, video, audio CD, CD-ROM, databases.

It houses more than 250,000 documents (including books, magazines, multimedia documents), thus being the largest public library with open shelves in Italy.

When exiting the library, the building you see is the:

PALAZZO RE ENZO

Piazza del Nettuno - Piazza Re Enzo   UTILITY

(i) it can only be visited on the occasion of exhibitions and events;

(bus) line n. 11, 13, 14,17, 18, 19, 20, 25, 27, 29, 30 (Rizzoli) 86 (P.Roosvelt) A (P.Maggiore) B, BLQcAerobus (S.Pietro)

(access) good

It was erected in 1244 as an enlargement of the seat of the Municipality, the Palazzo del Podestà. In 1386 Antonio Di Vincenzo realized the "*Sala del* Trecento". The last floor was renovated by Giovanni Giacomo Dotti in 1771, while in 1905 Alfonso Rubbiani *restored the Gothic aspect of the building.*

This became the rich prison of King Enzo of Sardinia, son of the Emperor Frederick II of Swabia. He was taken prisoner during the battle of Fossalta in 1249 and shut in by the Bologna's citizens until he died in 1272, so the palace was named after him.

Nowadays it is used for important congresses, conventions, shows, exhibitions and even convivial meetings, since the structure,

stretching over an area of 2,500 sq m, is multifunctional and able to hold numerous participants. In order to re-obtain his son, Frederick II is said to have offered such a long golden thread that it could surround the city's

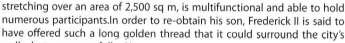

walls, but unsuccessfully. However, the young King Enzo was treated very honourably, and he even had a small royal court around him. Many stories are told on his period of imprisonment, some are true and some are legendary: from his love affaires with the Bologna's young ladies who competed to win his heart and bed, to his attempts to escape. One of the most famous attempts occurred in 1265, but he was discovered and taken prisoner again. This event is also represented in two tiles, unfortunately very corroded, situated in the side pillars of the Palazzo del Podestà. The remains of King Enzo are kept in the Basilica di San Domenico, where there are a gravestone and a relief portrait of him.

After the battle of Fossalta (1249), during which King Enzo was taken prisoner, almost all the seigniories of the Bologna's countryside had been defeated.

The ethical and economic consideration about the serfs, who until then had belonged to the Lords, occasioned fundamental changes. On August 25th 1256 the bell of Arengo placed on the Palazzo del Podestà summoned the Bologna's citizens to Piazza Maggiore: the city's governor (*Podestà*) and the People's Captain announced the liberation of about 6,000 serfs, belonging to about 400 lords (the Prendiparte family, proprietor of the homonymous tower, owned more than 200 serfs).

They were ransomed by the city's Treasury, that decided to take the disbursement and pay in Bologna's silver liras: 8 liras (for children) or 10 liras (for people older than 14 years); these were the market prices of the serfs. A fresco by Adolfo de Carolis kept in the hall of the Palazzo del Podestà represents this event. To free 5,855 serfs the Municipality paid 54,014 Bologna's liras.

The liberation of so many serfs, apparently due to ethical reasons, was primarily occasioned by economic interests: the Municipality expected a very probable better working performance of the serfs, as a consequence of their liberation, and planned also to extend the taxes to thousands of new individuals, who had been exempt until then.

Obviously, the Municipality wanted to take appropriate precautions and forbade the freed serfs to move outside of the diocese's area to which they belonged.

In some cases the serfs were gathered in certain free areas (which explains the origin of the names of some towns such as Castelfranco).

In the courtyard dividing the Palazzo del Podestà from the Palazzo Re Enzo sits the Cappella di Santa Maria dei Carcerati, that was a place of comfort and prayer for people condemned to death.

On the first floor there was the hangman's dwelling.

The Rota judges, whose offices were housed on the upper floor, complained in writing about the trouble people condemned to death caused to them when the hangman took and brought those people to the hanging execution, taking place on the railing of the Palazzo del Podestà.

PALAZZO DEL PODESTA'

🕂 **Piazza del Nettuno - Piazza Re Enzo**

ⓘ it can only be visited on the occasion of exhibitions and events;

🚌 line n. 11, 13, 14,17, 18, 19, 20, 25, 27, 29, 30 (Rizzoli) 86 (P.Roosvelt) A (P.Maggiore) B, BLQ Aerobus (S.Pietro) ♿ good

UTILITY

It was erected around 1200 by the new free Municipality, as public office building and thus seat of the *podestà*, the city's governor.

In consequence of transformations, the only remainder of the 13th century Romanesque style is the *Torre dello Arengo* (the so-called "campanone" (big bell), that at those times summoned the Bologna's citizens in event of danger, while nowadays on April 21st every year, to remind the citizens of the day in 1945 when the city was liberated from fascism).

The façade was designed by Aristotele Fioravanti – author of the Kremlin Palace in Moscow (where he was indicated as: Фиораванти, Фьораванти, Фиеравенти, Фиораванте).

In 1525 the terracotta statues of the city's patron saints by Alfonso Lombardi, Saint Petronius, Saint Proculus, Saint Dominic and Saint Francis, were placed under the vault (Voltone).

Under the *Voltone del Podestà* an extraordinary acoustic effect allows the visitors to talk to each other even in a low voice from the four opposite corners of the same vault.

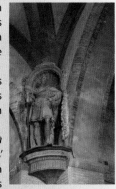

The lower part of the palace is decorated with hundredths of tiles having a floral motif, all different from each other.

Under the *Voltone del Podestà* there were also placed the notaries' desks, where people crowded on market days to register the contracts signed between private citizens, or the gallows for capital punishments, as you still can see by looking upwards to the section overlooking the square.

Exit the Voltone del Podestà and put your back to the Basilica di San Petronio, then look upwards and you will see the

TORRE RAMPONI

UTILITY

 via Rizzoli

line n. 11, 13, 14, 20, 27, 38, 39 (Rizzoli)

On the corner between Via Rizzoli and Via Fossalta, if you carefully look at the plasters of the 20th century palaces, it is possible to see the remains of the Torre Ramponi.

This was an important and powerful family belonging to the Guelph faction. Their tower overlooked the ancient "Mercato di Mezzo", the most important medieval city market.

Amongst the exponents of this family there were not only bold warriors, but also distinguished university professors.

The prestige of this family was so great that in 1251, when Pope Innocent IV came back from Lyon and passed by through Bologna (then he also stayed in Perugia for several months before going back to Rome, so waiting until the situation in the capital was safer), the Ramponi family played host to some Cardinals being part of the papal retinue.

Put your back to the Torre Ramponi and still look upwards, the tower you will see on the left corner of the Palazzo Re Enzo is the:

TORRE LAMBERTINI

📍 **via Rizzoli**

🚌 line n. 11, 13, 14, 19, 25, 28, 29, 30 (Rizzoli) 20, 27, A, B (S.Pietro)

UTILITY

It is located above the Palazzo Re Enzo and can be seen from Via Rizzoli. In 1294 the Municipality of Bologna felt it was necessary to have new spaces to satisfy the increased needs of the government. So it added the Casatorre Lambertini to the "Palatium Vetus", corresponding approximately to the current Palazzo del Podestà, and to the "Palatium Novum", corresponding to the current Palazzo Re Enzo.

This tower was acquired from the homonymous and powerful family, belonging to the Guelph faction and also famous for having captured King Enzo, son of the Emperor Frederick II. The interior spaces were first used by the People's Captain, a city's magistrate, and then as a prison, that initially was reserved to women and afterwards housed the high administrative officials.

In the glorious battle of Fossalta, which occurred on May 26th 1249, Lambertino di Guido together with an exponent of Bottrigari family and an exponent of Orsi family, disarmed and captured King Enzo, son of the Emperor Frederick II.

Go towards the Piazza Maggiore, the building you see on your left, right in front of the Palazzo Comunale, is the

PALAZZO DEI BANCHI

Piazza Maggiore;

UTILITY

line n. 11, 13, 14, 17, 18, 19, 20, 25, 27, 29, 30 (Rizzoli) 86 (P.Roosvelt) A (P.Maggiore) B, BLQ Aerobus (S.Pietro)

It was erected in 1412 and was named after the money changers' benches, that during the 15th and 16th centuries occupied the places in which today there are the shops.

In 1565 Jacopo Barozzi, called the Vignola, designed the façade as we currently see it, in order to hidden the not so attractive, even if typical, assemblage of medieval shops and houses overlooking the square, that still today can be seen beyond the porch.

And in front of you stands the

BI-10-1
MP3

BASILICA DI SAN PETRONIO

📍 **Piazza Maggiore** ☎ +39.051.225442   UTILITY

🕐 Winter 7.30-12.30 and 15-18; Summer 7.45-12.30 and 15.30-18. During the church services, the sightseeing could be limited or suspended. The hours can be subject to slight changes. **Museo di San Petronio:** tue-fri 9.30-12.30 and 15-17; Saturday 9.30-12.30; Sunday 15-17; ⓘ free; 🚌 line n. 11, 13, 14, 17, 18, 19, 20, 25, 27, 29, 30 (Rizzoli) 86 (P.Roosvelt) A (P.Maggiore) B, BLQ Aerobus (S.Pietro) ♿ very limited

This is the main church of Bologna, dedicated to the city's Patron Saint who was bishop here in the 5th century. The building dates back to 1390 and has a Gothic style. The works lasted a long time and were supervised by several architects, such as Baldassarre Peruzzi, Jacopo Barozzi da Vignola, Andrea Palladio and Alberto Alberti.

The decorations of the central nave were made by Girolamo Rinaldi, while the main portal with *"stories of the Old and New Testament"* and, in the lunette, an image of *"Mary and the Christ Child"*, were executed by Jacopo della Quercia.

It had immediately such a great prestige that Charles V chose it for its coronation by Clement VII. Actually this event could not take place in Rome, since it had been recently destroyed by the Landsknechts in the famous sack of Rome, during which the city was plundered and pillaged. Only from

the year 2000 it holds the relics of the patron saint, that until that moment were kept in the Chiesa di Santo Stefano.

Inside visitors can admire: *"The Mystic Marriage of Saint Catherine"* by Filippo Lippi, *"Madonna and Saints"* by Lorenzo Costa il giovane, and a *"Pietà"* by Amico Aspertini.

The stained glass windows generate a fascinating colour effect, while the *"Wooden Chorus"*, made by Agostino De Marchi in the 15th century, *"2 monumental organs"*, one of which executed by Lorenzo di Giacomo da Prato, and the *"Ciborium"* of the main altar, erected by Vignola in 1547, create a harmonious whole.

Almost all walls were frescoed by Giovanni da Modena and represent the journey of the Magi and episodes from the *"life of Saint Petronius"*.

The left wall represents the Last Judgement in a Dantesque style: namely, it contains *"the Paradise"*, place of the saints, and the *"Hell"* divided into pits with a large figure of Lucifer and Mohammed lying down. Visitors can also admire the *"Sundial"* by Giandomenico Cassini. The Church keeps the remains of Elisa Bonaparte, sister of Napoleon.

It seems that the Muslim fundamentalists did not appreciate the position assigned to Mohammed, and recently it became known that they planned an outrage in the Church.

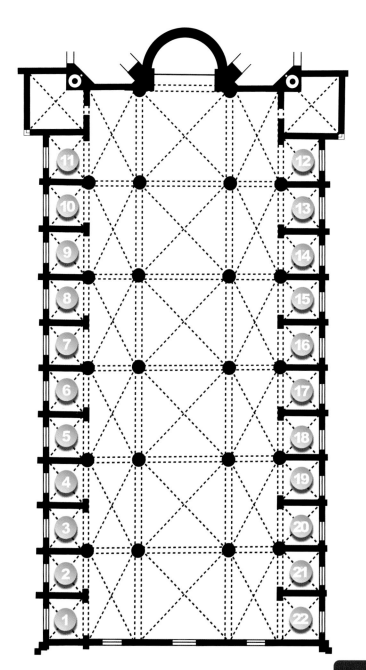

The twenty-two chapels that open off the side naves contain:

LEFT SIDE

1. <u>Cappella di S. Abbondio</u>, formerly Cappella dei Dieci di Balia. In 1865 it was restored by Albino Riccardi, who introduced a false Gothic style. Amongst the ancient elements there remain the ornamental decoration with the coats of arms of the patron saints (1397) and two large frescoes retouched by Giovanni da Modena (1420): on the right *"Triumph of the Catholic Church over Heresy"* and on the left *"Redemption of the original sin"*; in 1530 Pope Clement VII crowned there Charles V.

2. <u>Cappella di S. Petronio</u>, formerly Cospi e Aldrovandi, designed by Alfonso Torreggiani, intended to hold the relics of the head of Saint Petronius.

3. <u>Cappella di S. Ivo</u>, formerly Cappella di S. Brigida dei Foscherari: *statues* by Angelo Piò and paintings *"Madonna of Saint Luke and Saints Emidius and Ivo"* by Gaetano Gandolfi and *"Apparition of the Virgin to Saint Frances of Rome"* by Alessandro Tiarini (1615). On the pillar two clocks are present, that were almost the first ones to feature the pendulum correction in Italy (1758).

4. <u>Cappella dei Re Magi</u>, formerly Cappella Bolognini: Gothic marble barrier designed by Antonio di Vincenzo (1400); <u>on the altar</u> there is a wooden *"Polyptych"* with twenty-seven carved figures and other painted figures, artwork by Jacopo di Paolo. <u>The walls</u> were *frescoed* by Giovanni da Modena with a cycle representing:

<u>on the back wall</u>; *"Episodes from the life of Saint Petronius"*, *"Stories of the Magi"*,

<u>on the right wall</u>, *"The Last Judgement"*;

<u>on the left wall</u>, the *"Coronation of the Virgin"* in almond;

<u>at the top</u>, *"The Paradise and the Hell"*;

<u>at the bottom</u>, Dantesque-type representation, with a huge figure of Lucifer.

5. <u>Cappella di S. Sebastiano</u>, formerly Vaselli. There visitors can admire the large tempera painting *"Martyrdom of Saint Sebastian"*, and *"the Announced"* and the *"twelve Apostles"* executed on canvas by Lorenzo Costa; while the *"Announcing Angel"* is attributed to Francesco Francia;

6. <u>Cappella di S. Vincenzo Ferrer</u>, formerly Griffoni, Cospi e Ranuzzi: *bronze monument* representing the Cardinal Giacomo Lercaro executed by Giacomo Manzù (1954).

7. <u>Cappella di S. Giacomo</u>, formerly Rossi e Baciocchi: on the altar there is the *"Madonna on the Throne"*, masterpiece by Lorenzo Costa (1492); the designs on the stained glass windows are also attributed to the same author. *Funeral monument* with the remains of Prince Felice Baciocchi and his wife Elisa Bonaparte (1845);

8. <u>Cappella di S. Rocco</u>, formerly Ranuzzi: *"Saint Rocco"* by Parmigianino (1527). The large marble statue of *"Saint Petronius"* was executed by Gabriele Brunelli (1683). <u>The glass windows</u> were designed by Achille

Casanova (1926).

9. <u>Cappella di S. Michele</u> formerly Barbazzi e Manzoli: it houses the painting *"The Archangel Michael chasing the devil away"* by Donato Creti (1582).

10. <u>Cappella di S. Rosalia</u>, formerly dei Sedici del Senato, now del Municipio: it houses the canvas *"Glory of Saint Barbara"* by Alessandro Tiarini.

11. <u>Cappella di S. Bernardino</u>: shutters of the 15th century organ case by Lorenzo da Prato, painted by Amico Aspertini in 1531 with *"Four stories of Saint Petronius"*.

IN THE MIDDLE

<u>Cappella Maggiore</u>: on the altar there is a 15th century wooden *"Crucifix"*. At the back of the apse is the fresco *"Madonna with Saint Petronius"* by Marcantonio Franceschini and Luigi Quaini, based on cartoons by Cignani (1672). The ciborium on the main altar was erected by Vignola in 1547.

ON THE RIGHT SIDE

12. <u>Cappella delle Reliquie</u>, formerly Zambeccari, that represents the base for the bell tower.

13. <u>Cappella di S. Pietro Martire</u>, formerly della Società dei Beccari, with marble barrier executed by Francesco di Simone (end of 15th century);

14. <u>Cappella di S. Antonio da Padova</u>, formerly Saraceni e Cospi: statue of *"Saint Anthony of Padua"* attributed to Jacopo Sansovino.

15. <u>Cappella del Santissimo</u>, Malvezzi Campeggi, remade in the 19th century.

16. <u>Cappella dell'Immacolata</u>, formerly Fantuzzi: art nouveau decorations by Achille Casanova.

17. <u>Cappella di San Girolamo</u>, formerly Castelli: on the altar there is *"Saint Gerolamus"* attributed to Lorenzo Costa.

18. <u>Cappella di S. Lorenzo</u>, formerly Garganelli, Ratta e Pallotti: it houses the famous *Pietà* by Amico Aspertini.

19. <u>Cappella della Croce</u>, formerly dei Notai: devotional frescoes with *"Saints"* by Francesco Lola, Giovanni da Modena and Pietro Lianori (15th century). <u>The glass window</u> was executed by the blessed friar Giacomo da Ulma based on a design by Michele di Matteo.

20. <u>Cappella di S. Ambrogio</u>, formerly Marsili: *fresco* in Vivarini's style (middle of 15th century).

21. <u>Cappella di S. Brigida</u>, formerly Pepoli: *polyptych* by Tommaso Garelli (1477).

22. <u>Cappella della Madonna della Pace</u>: *"Madonna"* made of Istria stone and realized by Giovanni Ferabech (1394).

The bell tower, dating back to the second half of the 13th century, houses an assembly of 4 bells of the 15th century. They are manually rung by the city's bell associations, according to an ancient technique that is called Bologna's technique (the bell are all fastened to only one pin and turned 360°, thus eliminating the swaying movement that they otherwise would produce with enormous danger for the structural stability).

The consecration: On October 3rd 1954, namely on the Sunday preceding the feast of Saint Petronius, Cardinal Lercaro, archbishop of Bologna, solemnly consecrated the Basilica di San Petronio to worship. The announcement relative to the consecration took the Bologna's citizens by surprise, since they considered the church as having been already consecrated centuries ago, given that religious ceremonies had been taking place there for centuries. In fact, to hold religious ceremonies the church has only to have been blessed, while the consecration, representing the final act through which the church is eternally offered to God, can be deferred.

There exist two reasons for the delay. In the first place, the church has never been really completed: it is sufficient to consider the part of the section ending towards the Portico del Pavaglione and to observe the marble facing of the façade, that is interrupted at the height of the main door. The other reason is that the church belonged to the city's government. Only the Concordat of 1929 started the transfer of property to the Diocese, that was completed in 1937.

After exiting the Basilica, the building immediately adjacent to it on the left is the

PALAZZO DEI NOTAI

☎ **Via de' Pignattari, 1** 📞 +39.051.229858   **UTILITY**

ⓘ there can be visited: "Sala dei Notai" only on the occasion of exhibitions and events; 🚌 line n. 20, 28, A, B, BLQ (S.Pietro) 25, 29, 30, (Rizzoli) 17, 18, 86 (P. Roosvelt)

This is one of the Bologna's historic buildings, and was erected in 1381 by the Notaries' society in order to have it as their seat.

This Palace was built in two different moments: the more ancient part overlooks the Cattedrale di San Petronio, and was erected in 1381 under the direction of Berto Cavalletto and Lorenzo da Bagnomarino. It underwent several renovations, some of which were material, such as the creation of six pierced windows decorated with small columns, that were executed by Antonio di Vincenzo in 1385.

The more recent part, overlooking Via d'Accursio, underwent modifications by Bartolomeo Fioravanti around 1437.

During some centuries the Palace maintained its appearance until when, in 1908, Alfonso Rubbiani entirely renovated it and also had his coat of arms placed on the main façade.

Inside visitors can admire valuable *frescoes* dating back to the 14th century, and the Notaries' coat of arms representing "three inkwells with quill feathers on a red background".

Take Via IV Novembre, that is the road running along the wall of the Palazzo Comunale, and after reaching the end of the wall you will see the tower serving nowadays as entrance passage, namely the

TORRE LAPI

 UTILITY

 Via 4 Novembre
 line n. 17, 18, 86 (P. Roosvelt)

It is deemed to have been part of the first "circle" of the walls (4th century AD), thus having been erected as entrance passage.

Then it was acquired by Lapi noble family, which adapted it to their needs. In the 14th century the Bologna's municipality bought it for 400 liras, because they felt the necessity of enlarging the Palazzo Comunale.

Over the centuries it underwent several modifications, amongst which one of the last ones was the reduction of the height to the current 18 metres approximately, that was realized during the Napoleon's epoch. Moreover, the entrance passage to the seat of the Palazzo Comunale was reopened in 1948. (Previously it had been closed, and this is the reason why the tower did not blow up in the 17th century, when a fire burnt up and affected the nearby Torre Agresti).

A CURIOUS NOTE

In the second half of the 14th century, the city's government wanted to free the Piazza Maggiore from the meat dealers, so stimulated them to move to the current Via IV Novembre, while on the tower base a shop was specifically created, which later was rented out to a "beccaio" (i.e. a butcher).

However, after some decades, in 1505 the Bologna's Senate, annoyed by the smells and dirt occasioned by the market adjacent to the Palazzo Comunale, decided to free all the area from benches, shops and sheds and, at the same time, had the opening on the tower base closed.

TORRE DEGLI AGRESTI

UTILITY

 Piazza Galileo Galilei

line n. 17, 18, 86 (P. Roosvelt)

The Agresti family is one of the less known of the Bologna's ancient noble families. Their tower is embedded amongst the modern buildings overlooking the Piazza Galilei, a square that has been enlarged through demolitions occurred at the beginning of the century, and as a consequence of the second world war bombing.

Originally it must have been higher, if you consider the thickness of the walls on the base, but later its height was reduced to the current 20 metres with the execution of a turret, while there were removed the traditional selenite blocks, that were peculiar to the base of Bologna's towers.

A CURIOUS NOTE

In the night of August 2nd 1641 a strong fire broke out in the shop of a brass worker at the tower foot, and affected the nearby buildings. Wood, so widespread for construction at that time, kept on blazing supported by the wind that fanned the flames, while people tried to restrain the fire with great difficulty.

Panic spread when the flames fed by the wind approached the "Torre Lapi" (embedded today in the complex of the Palazzo Comunale) that once was a warehouse containing munitions and gunpowder.

Fortunately the situation took a turn for the better, the fire was extinguished and the "Collegio di Spagna", being the owner of the tower at that time, paid for the huge reconstruction expenses.

PALAZZO CAPRARA

via IV Novembre, 22;
line n. 17, 18, 86 (P.Roosvelt)

UTILITY

This palace was built for want of the count Girolamo Caprara in 1603, and is traditionally attributed to Francesco Terribilia.

Then it was completed in 1705 according to a design of Giuseppe Antonio Torri and his pupil Alfonso Torreggiani; the grand staircase is also attributed to Antonio Laghi.

On the noble floor are housed some beautiful tempera paintings by Pietro Paltronieri (called the Mirandolese), Vittoria Maria Bigari (dating back to 1720 approximately) and Bernardo Minozzi.

In 1805 the building played host to Napoleon, who acquired the palace in the following year.

Today it is the seat of the Bologna's Prefecture.

Carlo Montecuccoli Caprara was born as son of the count Niccolò and the Florentine Donna Ippolita Virginia Salviati on September 12th 1755. He is told to have been a man characterized by the desire of excelling and inclined to do.

He stood out as the main representative of Bologna's Senate in Napoleon's circle, and decisively accepted the changes Napoleon introduced in the city's organization.He was able to be assigned several titles, however occupied few prominent offices.

Guidicini describes him as a "magnificent, splendid, generous and good hearted man", which led him to use up his huge personal assets. In 1806 Napoleon acquired from him the building located at Via IV Novembre, including all the internal furniture, by paying a symbolic amount of money. This did not correspond to the real value, but was actually aimed at giving this noble Caprara the possibility to honour the several debts he had incurred.

Keep on going along Via IV Novembre, and the building you will see on your right, on the corner with the Piazza Roosvelt, is the

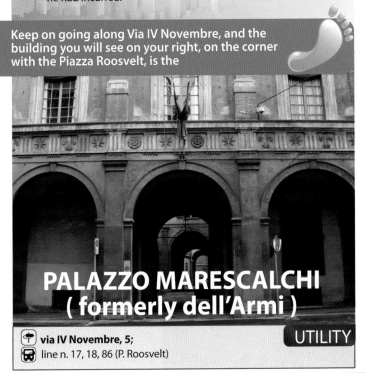

PALAZZO MARESCALCHI
(formerly dell'Armi)

via IV Novembre, 5;

line n. 17, 18, 86 (P. Roosvelt)

UTILITY

39

It was erected on account of Aurelio dell'Armi around 1466, and was remade around 1613. The design is attributed to the architect Floriano Ambrosiani.

Inside:

<u>on the ground floor</u> there are *frescoes* by G. Cavedoni and Valesio

<u>on the noble floor</u> *two frescoed chimneys* are kept: one featuring the "*Vigilance*" by L. Carracci and the other featuring the "*Medea's incantation*" (probable work by L. Sabbatini) with *statues* by G. Tedeschi; besides, there are halls containing *frescoes* by F. Brizio, A. Tiarini, G. Reni. In 1811 Ferdinando Marescalchi entrusted the decoration of the oval dining hall to F. Giani, who embellished it very elegantly.

A CURIOUS NOTE

A great Pope, Gregory XIII, was descended from a branch of this family. His real name was Ugo Boncompagni, and was born as son of Cristoforo Boncompagni and Angela Marescalchi in 1502. In more recent times, Ferdinando Marescalchi, a senator having noble origins and living in Bologna during the papal dominion, was fascinated by the new ideas coming from France, thus becoming their fervent supporter.

He was co-opted onto the new institutions and, after occupying prominent offices in the city's internal government, became Minister of the Foreign Relationships of Italian Republic, and later of the Kingdom of Italy, and as such he lived in Paris from 1802 to 1814.

Keep on going along Via IV Novembre again, to reach the crossing where immediately on the left is the flight of steps leading to the

CHIESA DI SS.SALVATORE

UTILITY

📍 **via C. Battisti**

☎ +39.051. 222.852

🕐 working days 7-14 and 16-19.30 ♿ very limited

🚌 line n. 17, 18, 86 (P.Roosvelt) 11, 20, 25, 27, 29, 30 (Rizzoli) A, B (S.Pietro)

It was the seat of the canons of Santa Maria di Reno until 1100.

The current <u>building</u>, with the exception of the Romanesque bell tower, dates back to 1623 and was realized by A. Mazenta.

<u>Inside</u> visitors can admire *statues* by G. Tedeschi, C. Molli; *paintings* by Simone de' Crocifissi, Vitale da Bologna, Garofalo, Innocenzo da Imola, J. Coppi, G. Cavedoni, Mastelletta, Girolamo da Treviso, Girolamo da Carpi, G. F. Gessi, A. Tiarini, C. Bodoni.

<u>The sacristy</u> goes back to the 17th century.

<u>The adjoining former Convento</u> di San Salvatore, that dates back to 1512 and was damaged by bombings in 1943, holds three cloisters going back to the 15th and 16th centuries.

A CURIOUS NOTE

Several churches kept once a strange register: the "Necrologio" (the Necrology). This was a kind of calendar stating on each day the names of the dead, whether brethren or laics, for whom to pray.

Therefore, the Necrologio had a liturgical and administrative function simultaneously since, besides the names, it also contained the amount of the legacy donated both for future remembrance and as an implied invitation to appropriately use it.Between 1167 and 1173, an unknown canon entered most of the deaths; then this job was continued by one of his brothers, who seemingly invited people to pray in proportion to the received legacy.In the 13th century, in the "Necrologio Renano" the administrative function seems to become more and more significant, since it aimed at remembering the donations received.

After exiting the church, in front of you you will see a road intersecting with Via C.Battisti and called Via Porta Nova, take it and walk ahead until you pass under the

TORRESOTTO
DI VIA PORTA NUOVA

Piazza Malpighi
line n. 11, 13, 14, 20, 21, 29, 30, D (P.Malpighi)

UTILITY

The *Torresotto*[1] or *Serraglio* (small tower) *di Porta Nova* belongs to the second circle of the walls, which is actually called *Cerchia dei Torresotti* or, improperly, *del Mille*.

Notes:
[1] *Bologna was surrounded by three circles of walls.*
*The second one was started in the late 12th century, and it was called Cerchia **dei Torresotti** due to the presence of fortified structures located close to the doors.*

In the middle of the square, right in front of you, there is the

COLONNA DELL'IMMACOLATA

UTILITY

Piazza Malpighi
line n. 11, 13, 14, 20, 21, 29, 30, D (P.Malpighi)

It was designed by F. Dotti, with copper statues by Giovanni Tedeschi (1638), according to a drawing attributed to Guido Reni.

After passing under the Torresotto, cross the road and go towards the right side, then turn around the basilica by keeping it on your left side, now admire its architecture until the entrance to the

BI-19
MP3

BASILICA DI SAN FRANCESCO

🪧 **Piazza S. Francesco**   ☎ +39.051.221762   **UTILITY**
🕐 6.30 -12 and 15-19; ♿ limited; 🚌 line n. 11, 13, 14, 20, 21, 29, 30, D (P.Malpighi)

It stands on Piazza San Francesco.

This church was built for want of the Bologna's Franciscan community, and is dedicated to Saint Francis of Assisi *"the Poor Man"*.

Its construction was started around 1236 by Marco Brescia and his brother Giovanni, who was a Franciscan friar.

<u>The façade</u> dates back to 1250 and features a Romanesque-Gothic style.

<u>The interior</u> is divided into three naves with an apse deambulatory and a crown of nine radial chapels.

<u>The vaults</u> are extremely high and divided into six sails with sharp and rampant arches on the buttresses.

<u>On the main altar</u> there is a large marble altar-piece executed by Jacobello and Pier

Paolo delle Masegne and dating back to 1393.

The sacristy was realized according to a design by Antonio Di Vincenzo.

Inside, the Basilica houses the mortal remains of Anti-Pope Alexander V, a 15th century artwork by Nicolò Lamberti and Sperandino.

The Cappella di San Bernardino, executed by Antonio di Vincenzo, the Cappella Muzzarelli and the main bell tower, containing a fresco by Pietro di Giovanni Lianori, date back to the 15th century. Along the southern side of the church, visitors will find the *Chiostro dei Morti*, dating back to the 14th century and holding several tombs of Studio's rectors.

The church was deconsecrated by the French in 1798 and transformed into Customs House. In 1886 it was consecrated again and in 1928 it underwent restoration works. During the Second World War it suffered bombings.

Outside, behind the apse, there are the notably interesting funerary monuments of the glossers "Accursio" and his "son Francesco d'Accursio", dating back to 1258. The third tomb belongs to Rolandino dei Romanzi, while the tomb located in the middle belongs to the jurist "Odofredo" and dates back to 1265. He had a profitable carrier as a lawyer, then he became university professor. He is known to have made a famous argumentative statement against people who considered his lessons as being too

expensive: "All people want to learn, but no-one wants to know the price of the learning".

Exit the Basilica from the left side door (looking at the main altar), cross the road and walk ahead until you reach the crossing with Via del Pratello, then turn left, continue straight until you reach Via de' Coltellini on the right, take this road and continue straight to the end, where it crosses with Via S.Felice, turn left, cross the road and walk ahead until you reach Via dell'Abbadia on the right, take this road and, after a while, on the right you will see the

EX MONASTERO DEI SS. NABORRE E FELICE DETTO ABBADIA

UTILITY

 via dell'Abbadia, 1

 line n. 13, 19, 36, 38, 39

(S.Felice)

It is presumed to have been the city's first Episcopal seat at the time of the Proto-bishop Saint Zama. The building seems to have been renovated and enlarged by Bishop Faustiniano and then by Bishop Felice during the 5th century, when it was dedicated to the martyrs Nabor and Felix. Bishop Felice was buried there, besides he was so worshipped that the church was named after him.

The reorganization carried out by the Benedictine monks, who settled there in 1110, left its traces on the outside of the ancient church, that was restored in 1950, and in the crypt underneath. Other ancient parts are the bell tower, dating back to the end of the 14th century, and a cloister with double open gallery, going back to the 15th century. In 1512 the Poor Clares acquired the property of the church, but not of the other parts of the complex. Although the monastery had some

real estates, it had initially poor economic resources also because of the steady increase of the nuns. Actually, towards the end of the 16th century it houses about one hundred professed nuns.

The Poor Clares made some restorations, that were executed according to the taste of those times and gave to the church the appearance it still preserves today. The building was modified by lifting the floor and raising the Romanesque perimeter walls; moreover, a cupola was added. The crypt, that was separated from the church, became a chapel inside the monastery, while a belfry was added to the bell tower.

From 1868 it has been Military Hospital.*From 1868 it has been Military Hospital.*

Go back to Via S.Felice, turn left and walk back towards the city's centre. Continue straight ahead and, at the end of the road, cross the road and keep on ahead along Via U.Bassi, the second road on the left is Via N.Sauro, keep it and continue ahead until the end of the church. Then if you look upward, you will see the

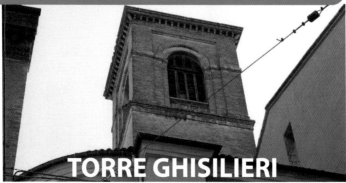

TORRE GHISILIERI

The bell tower of the Chiesa di San Gregorio e Siro is the tower Ghisilieri, dating back to the 13th century.

This family is one of the most distinguished, powerful, proud and quarrelsome ones in Bologna's history.

Many exponents of it occupied important administrative offices, some was beatified, several fought and shed their blood on the battlefield or on the scaffold.

A CURIOUS NOTE

The Ghislieri family, one of the city's most ancient noble families, seems to descend from a certain Ghisliero di Costantinopoli, who followed Saint Petronius up to Bologna, while going back from Constantinople with some relics.

Following the civil wars between Guelphs and Ghibellines, this noble family, that belonged to the Guelph faction and defended the ecclesiastical interests, was chased away from Bologna with the confiscation of their whole property.

The future Pope Pius V was descended from a branch of this family who had taken refuge to Piemonte.

Continue straight along Via N.Sauro until it ends at Via Riva di Reno, then turn right and, at the end of the road, on your left you will see the

SANTUARIO DI SANTA MARIA DELLA PIOGGIA

UTILITY

⌖ **Via Riva Reno, 124 (ang. Via Avesella)**

☎ +39.051.223.885

🕔 7-12 and 16-19 approximate hours;

♿ limited 🚍 line n. 11, 17, 21, 25, 28, 30, 36, 38, 39 (Marconi)

The sanctuary is located on the crossing between Via Galliera and Via Riva di Reno, and recently it has undergone restoration both inside and on the frescoed façade.The church consists of a single nave with three lateral chapels on either side, and is covered by a frescoed barrel vault.

The complex, including the Oratorio di San Bartolomeo, early showed a caring vocation by creating spaces where to house foreigners travelling to Rome, and an orphanage for children orphaned by the plague and the consequent famine of 1527.

In 1561 Bologna suffered a severe drought; people gathered to pray and a procession was also organized, which is still remembered because heavy rains followed it. From then onwards, the cult of the Madonna della Pioggia began.

The artworks currently kept inside come from donations of the citizens, who intended to thank the church for its noble caring activity.

On the main altar of the church there is a small painting representing the *"Madonna and Child surrounded by seven angels' heads"*, that is attributed to the painter Michele di Matteo.

This small artwork is being worshipped for centuries. It was discovered in the 14th century, during the removal of the debris caused by the destruction in a fire of a palace adjacent to the oratory.

The finding is considered to be a miracle for two reasons: primarily because the work looked completely unharmed despite the dramatic vicissitudes it suffered, and secondarily because to it was attributed the miraculous healing of a blind man who had come to honour the rediscovered icon.

The collection includes very valuable artworks, among which visitors can admire three paintings by Agostino Carracci, cousin of Ludovico Carracci: *"Adoration of the shepherds"*, *"Altarpiece of Saint Bartholomew from Reno"* and the *"Two Prophets"* in the arch of the chapel.

Other works are: *"Saint Bartholomew"* by Francesco Monti; *"Madonna of Providence"*, namely a stone statue located on the left side of the altar; *"Christ crowned with thorns"*, *a polychrome terracotta bust* protected by a glass shrine; *"Saint Vincenzo Ferreri"* by Antonio Crespi and *"Saint Luigi Gonzaga"* by Ercole Graziani, *two framed oval paintings* located on either side of the altar; *"Saint Peter after his triple denial of Christ"*, *"Mystic marriage of Saint Catherine"* and the *"Burial of Saint Catherine from Alexandria"* attributed to Graziani and situated in the sacristy. On the right side of the altar visitors can admire: *"Camillo dè Lellis attending a sick man"* by Dante Bizzotto; a statue depicting *"Saint Anthony of Padua and Child"* by G.A. Raimondi; *"Madonna and Child enthroned with Saints Catherine and Lucy"*, a 16th century painting by Alessandro Stiatici.

THE FORMER ORATORY

At 124 Via Riva di Reno there is the access to the rooms leading to the first floor of the complex, which was formerly named after Saint Bartholomew from Reno and contained some halls of the orphanage and the oratory, seat of the Company of Saint Bartholomew. Visitors will go up a 18th century staircase, dominated by the beautiful *"Landscape with Saint Bartholomew"* by Ludovico Mattioli.

The halls house 16th century frescoes, and a particular terracotta sculpture executed by Alfonso Lombardi and depicting *"Saint Bartholomew"*.

The road you cross is Via Galliera, now turn right and the palace you will see at number 14 is the

PALAZZO
FELICINI

📍 **via Galliera, 14**   UTILITY
🚌 line n. 11, 27, A, B (Indipendenza) BLQ (Arena del Sole)

Its construction was commissioned by Bartolomeo Felicini in 1497, and it currently still maintains its original architecture almost entirely, even if the façade was renovated in 1906.

In 1561 it became a property of the Fibbia family and was enriched with important decorations, such as the "Allegory of Aurora", the "Triumph of Bacchus and Ariadne" and the "Twilight" by Domenico Maria Canuti and D. Santi, and the "Fall of Phaeton" and the "Assumption of the Virgin" by Angelo Michele Colonna and G. Alberesi. All these works date back to 1664.

Between the 14th and 15th centuries the Felicini family, that had important bankers in it at those times and also belonged to the rich landed aristocracy, built its dwelling "as if it were designed for a prince or a sovereign" (so the chronicler Borselli described it).

Following the decline of their fortune, the palace was initially handed over to Cardinal Pucci, and then to the Fibbia family.

In this palace they housed many famous guests, who included, in 1515, the King of France Francis I, who was accompanied by Leonardo da Vinci and Filiberta of Savoy.

According to legend, Leonardo seems to have realized his Mona Lisa in this Bologna's house, thus drawing his inspiration from Filiberta of Savoy and not from Lisa di Francesco Giocondo, as tradition states.

Keep on walking along this road until you reach, on your right, the

PALAZZO ALDROVANDI MONTANARI

via Galliera, 8

UTILITY

line n. 20, 38 (S.Pietro) 38, 39 (Marconi)

This ancient palace Aldrovandi, later handed over to the Montanari family, stands in the heart of Bologna's historic centre among other important ancient buildings.This was the aristocratic residence of the Aldrovandi family, and then it became the governmental seat of the Papal Legate Cardinal Pompeo Aldrovandi. Its construction was started by Francesco Maria Angelini in 1725, who designed the staircase on the ground floor and the entrance hall. Afterwards, Alfonso Torreggiani was entrusted to complete it, and in 1752 the grand staircase and the façade were finished.

The interior is enriched with *frescoes* by Vittorio Maria Bigari who, with the cooperation of the painter of *quadrature* Stefano Orlandi, decorated the vault of the grand staircase in 1722, the entrance hall in 1728, the main hall in 1748 and the gallery of the statues in 1755 (that originally housed a collection of Roman busts with representations, among other, of the glorious events of this noble linege).The palace underwent a remarkable scientific renovation work and technological updating, that aimed at adapting it according to the most excellent current standards, with the full consent of the guardianship of the Ministry of Cultural Heritage, to which it is subject.

A CURIOUS NOTE

The Aldrovandi family is a Bologna's ancient aristocratic family, that over the centuries acquired a considerable land assets in city's province, besides several buildings located in Bologna in the area of Via Galliera, thanks to marriage dowries, acquisitions, emphyteusis and inheritances.

Among the most energetic exponents of this family, Cardinal Pompeo Aldrovandi (1668 - 1752) must be remembered, who also contended with another Bologna's citizen, Cardinal Lambertini, for the tiara. Afterwards, the latter ascended the papal throne taking the name of Pope Benedict XIV.

During the conclave Lambertini seems to have said to the cardinals: «If you desire to elect a saint, choose Gotti; if you want to elect a statesman, choose Aldrovandi (Cardinal Pompeo Marescotto-Aldrovandi); instead, if you want a donkey, elect me».

It is curious to remember that a large quantity of bricks used to build the Bologna's Palazzo Aldrovandi Montanari was manufactured in the kilns of Mirabello, and conveyed to Bologna along the Naviglio up to the current Via del Porto nearby, the toponym of which indicates the function this place had at those times, before the canal was filled in.

While continuing straight along this road, the second road on the left is Via Manzoni, take it and, after a while, on your left you will see the

CHIESA MADONNA DI GALLIERA

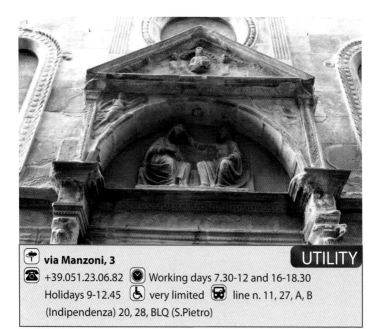

via Manzoni, 3

UTILITY

+39.051.23.06.82　Working days 7.30-12 and 16-18.30
Holidays 9-12.45　very limited　line n. 11, 27, A, B
(Indipendenza) 20, 28, BLQ (S.Pietro)

It was erected at the beginning of the 14th century and was reconstructed during the period 1479-92, when a miraculous image of *"Madonna and Child"* was moved to the main altar. Originally it was frescoed under a portico next to the church.In 1510 the new façade was erected according to a design by Donato di Gaio da Cernobbio, and was embellished by elegant sandstone reliefs, that are currently really damaged.

In 1622 it was granted to the Fathers of the Congregation of Saint Philip Neri, and in 1684 it was enlarged and renovated in the interior. On the altar there are valuable sculptures and paintings, among which the most noteworthy are the *"The ecstasy of Saint Philip"* by Guercino and the decoration of the *main chapel* by Francesco Maria Galli Bibiena.Moreover, the interior houses also frescoes by Giuseppe Marchesi, executed in 1730; paintings by Francesco Albani, A. M. Colonna, L. Pasinelli, T. Muratori, G. Donnini, M. A. Franceschini and sculptures by G. Mazza (about 1695) A. G. Piò (1740), S. Giannotti (1741).

A CURIOUS NOTE

The Order of the Oratorians, or *"Filippini"*, was founded by Saint Philip Neri in Rome in 1575 as Congregation of the Oratory, with the papal bull "Copiosus in misericordia" issued by Gregory XIII. Then it was approved by Paul V in 1612 and confederated in 1942. In Bologna's Diocese, the Fathers obtained the Chiesa della Madonna di Galliera from Cardinal Ludovisi who, after he had become Pope taking the name of Gregory XV, approved the Bologna's Congregation of the Oratory in 1621.

The Napoleonic suppression in 1806 and the Italian Government's suppression in 1866, took away from the Fathers their large convent and all their assets.

Right in front of the church there is the

BI-06
MP3

PALAZZO GHISLARDI- FAVA
Museo Civico Medioevale

UTILITY

Via Manzoni, 4
+39.051.2193916
Musei Civici d'Arte Antica:
Tue-Fri 9-15, Sat-Sun and holydays 10-18.30, closed: Monday (if not holiday) January 1st, May 1st, December 25th, early closing at 14: December 24th and 31st (i) free (excepting on the occasion of exhibitions)
(good) line 11, 27, 28, A, B (Indipendenza), 20, BLQ Aerobus (S.Pietro)

The area in which the palace stands is especially interesting on a historical and archaeological level, since it still keeps some ruins of the "Palatium Vetus", that was completely destroyed by the Bologna's citizens in 1115 because of it being the symbol of the oppression of imperial power.

Inside the museum, visitors can admire works belonging to Longobard production and a bronze ewer of Saxon origin. The museum houses also a copper statue representing "Boniface VIII" and a collection of codices and books, that testifies to the Bologna's miniature tradition. Besides, there are several ceramic pieces, glass pieces and musical instruments, as well as a collection of arms.

Palazzo Ghisilardi-Fava is a Bologna's medieval palace located at Via Manzoni, which today houses the Museo Civico Medievale of Bologna.

It was built between 1484 and 1491, and fully represents the architectural model typical of the period dominated by the Bentivoglio family. At that time, the Fava family owned a part of the homonymous palace and the Chiesa della Madonna di Galliera, attributed to Antonio Morandi.

In the courtyard of the palace stands the "Torre dei Conoscenti" (13th century). It was built before the palace and features the typical characteristics of a *casa-torre* ("house-tower", i.e., a building having simultaneously a housing and defensive function). It has the particularity to have been missed in the census of the city's towers, and nowadays it is known as the rediscovered tower.

Incredibly, only the renovation of 1975, which was executed with the purpose of moving there the Museo Civico, proceeded to tear down the two floors added on the western wing of the complex, thus revealing the tower that now stands again over the palace roof.

After exiting the museum, turn right and continue straight until you cross Via Indipendenza, there turn right and, after a few steps, you will be in the starting point, which is the end of this tour.

TOUR

2

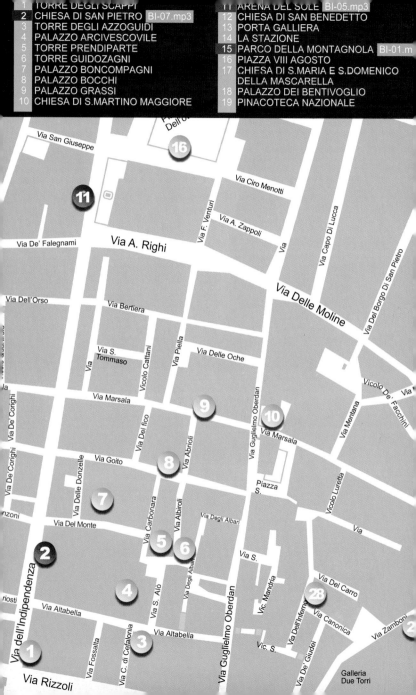

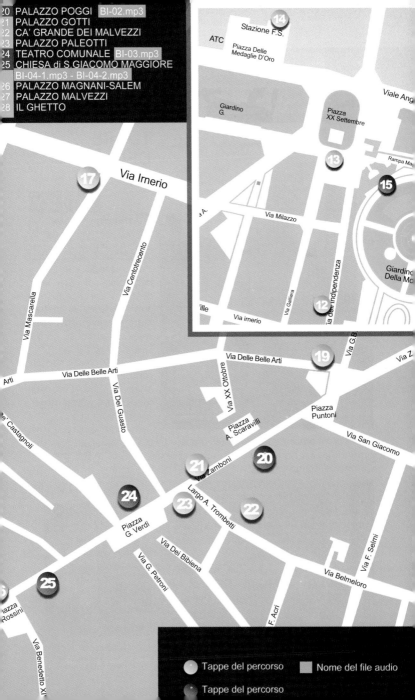

This tour also starts from the heart of Bologna; reach Piazza Nettuno and, for the sake of convenience, stand up on the steps of the Biblioteca Sala Borsa. From there you will see the following tower standing over the roofs of the houses (but formerly it was not so)

TORRE DEGLI SCAPPI

UTILITY

via Indipendenza

line n. 11, 20, 27, A, B (S.Pietro)

It stands at the beginning of the very central Via Indipendenza and measures 39 metres high, however, to better see it, you must go to Piazza del Nettuno.

It would have had to compete with the nearby Altabella and Coronata towers, but it was never completed.

Today, the base of the tower is incorporated in the 16th century Casa Coccapani, and on the ground floor it houses one of the most ancient shops in Bologna, "La Coroncina", founded in 1694.

A CURIOUS NOTE

In the 19th century the "Canton dei Fiori", the corner between Via Rizzoli and Via Indipendenza, which was so called because of the presence of some flower shops, was occupied by a palace lower than the current house in false Renaissance style, that refers to the ancient toponym due to the decorations of the small balcony on the corner.

BI-07
MP3

UTILITY

📍 **Via Indipendenza, 9**
☎ +39.051.222112
🕐 8.30-12 and 16-18.15;
Museo della Cattedrale di San Pietro:
☎ +39.051.222112
🕐 Sat-Sun 16-17.30
(mornings reserved for schools by appointment), Mon-Fri only for groups by reservation;
ℹ️ free
♿ good (via Altabella 4)
🚌 line n. 20, 28, A, B, BLQ Aerobus (S.Pietro)

CHIESA DI SAN PIETRO

It has been the metropolitan cathedral of Bologna since 1582, being promoted as such

by Pope Gregory XIII. After many destructions it was definitely rebuilt in the 17th century on a design by Floriano Ambrosiani. Most probably, right from the 5th century the bishop

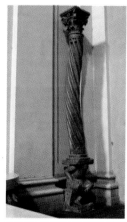

established here one of his residences. Actually, in the church a baptistery was placed and the poorhouse and the first college of priests and deacons were also housed.

Now the interior clearly presents a baroque appearance, thus giving the impression of great majesty.

Among the artworks, visitors can admire the Annunciation by Ludovico Carracci, frescoed in the central lunette of the presbytery, a Romanesque Crucifixion of cedar wood, and a terracotta sculptural group dating back to the 16th century, called Dead Christ with the mourning Maries, by Alfonso Lombardi.

The Ravenna-style cylindrical bell tower measures about 70 metres high, and today it is enclosed by the stately Romanesque belfry erected during the 12th – 13th centuries.

A CURIOUS NOTE

From 1575 onwards, the interior of the building was radically renovated by command of Cardinal Gabriele Paleotti.

These changes were so profound that they caused the collapse of the vaults in 1599.

After exiting the church, turn left and take the road running along the side of the church, Via Altabella, then, at the first corner, look to the right and you will see the

TORRE DEGLI AZZOGUIDI

via Altabella   UTILITY

line n. 20, 28, A, B, BLQ (S.Pietro) 11, 27 (Indipendenza) 25, 29, 30, (Rizzoli)

It is also called Torre Altabella, and is one of the about 20 aristocratic towers[1] still existing in the historic centre.

It was built in the second half of the 12th century and measures 61 metres high (thus being the Bologna's second highest tower after the Asinelli tower). It is also named *Altabella* because of its height, perfect verticality and elegance: at about 28 metres off the ground an offset is present, which reduces it laterally and makes its structure look notably slimmer.

The street where the tower currently stands, next to the Cattedrale di San Pietro, is called Altabella just in honour of its nickname.

The entrance door is surmounted by an ogival arch made of selenite ashlars, with two ornamental narrow stringcourses.

During the 19th century the base of the tower, that is faced with 10 rows of selenite parallelepipeds, was adapted in order to house a shop. The original door was enlarged, while the thickness of the internal walls was reduced so as to create space, thus greatly compromising the stability of the building. However, in the fifties years a renovation was carried out to strengthen it.

Notes

[1] *The reasons why so many towers were erected are still unclear, however many believe that, during the period of struggle for the pro-Emperor and pro-Pope investitures, the richest families used them as an offensive and/or defensive instrument, and* <u>*as a symbol of power*</u>*.*

The Azzoguidi family became known in Bologna from 1228. They belonged to the Guelph faction, but they were not really involved in the struggles affecting the city during the Middle Age.

Together with the Prendiparte family, they kept watch over the cathedral, thus constituting the protective belt for the Guelph power, which prevailed in Bologna's effective government during the 13th and 14th centuries.

Among its exponents there were several ambassadors and condottieri, especially in the 14th and 15th centuries, but also some scientists (such as Baldassarre, who was the first Bologna's typographer).

In front of the tower there is the

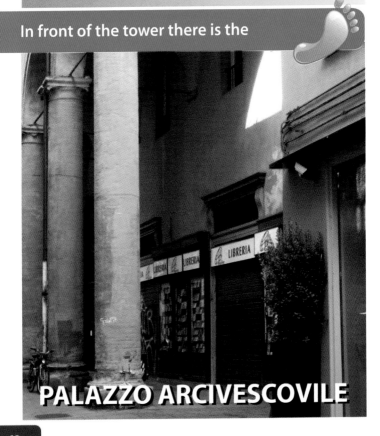

PALAZZO ARCIVESCOVILE

The high portico is dated back to the 13th century, and it is seemed to have been built for want of Bishop Enrico della Fratta; however, the four arches towards Via Sant'Alò were erected in the 16th century. The 16th century courtyard was realized by Domenico Ribaldi; in the middle of the 19th century, it underwent renovation work commissioned by Cardinal Oppizzoni. The entrance <u>vault</u> dates back to 1772.

<u>Inside</u> visitors can find architectural fragments going back to the 13th and 14th centuries. The *decorations of the chapel on the ground floor date back to 1790, and were executed by F. Minozzi, while the various halls on the upper floor were decorated by P. Fancelli and other artists in the 19th century.*

A CURIOUS NOTE

According to tradition, the Bologna's Cardinal Lambertini was known for his authoritativeness and, if necessary, sternness with which he dealt with the ecclesiastical matters, although he maintained his cheerful and jovial character.
(passage extracted from Botta, History of Italy, book XLI)
"After Marcellus II, who too soon left the Christendom, no-one who ascended the papal throne could be compared to Lambertini for intelligence and caution. He realized that the best way to keep his reasons is not to provoke his opponents. He was the Pope who that century wanted. The disputes with Rome ceased to create hostility, but they became discussions, while the disbelief, which unfortunately was spreading among the generations, stopped in front of an amiable and witty Pope".

Continue straight along this road until the first crossing where, on your left, there is Via S.Alò, take it and the tower you will see in front of you is the

TORRE PRENDIPARTE

UTILITY

 Piazzetta Sant'Alò, 7

🕐 it can be accessed only on the occasion of events and guided tours;

🚌 line n. 20, 28, A, B, BLQ (S.Pietro) 11, 27 (Indipendenza) 25, 29, 30, (Rizzoli)

It stands on a spot where the road enlarges and forms a kind of small square, that was known as Piazzetta di San Senesio because of the presence of an ancient church, now disappeared.

This tower is also called "Torre Coronata", since at about 50 metres off the ground there is an offset having a peculiar shape, which reduces its thickness. It is another one of the about 20 aristocratic towers[1] still existing in the historic centre.

It was erected in the second half of the 12th century, measures 59.50 metres high (61 metres if the pinnacle at the top is included), and is characterized by a slight slope. The thickness of the walls at the base (about 2.80 metres) suggests that the tower was very probably broken off, or it was not completed. Moreover, at the base the walls are faced with 9 rows of selenite parallelepipeds. On the only side completely free from houses, there are an original window, located at a height of about 20 metres, and two modern windows, located at a lower height. At the same height as the second modern window is a very much worn sandstone coat of arms, which is illegible (probably it dates back to the 15th century).

The Prendiparte family, belonging to the Guelph faction, goes back to 1154, and it is remembered among the city's noble families. Two of its members were consuls of Bologna during the 12th century, while in the 13th century exponents of the Prendiparte family were appointed 13 times as Podestà (i.e., governor) in several Italian cities. The tower was first sold in 1293, however the Prendiparte family regained its possession. Then, they finally sold it in the 15th century, when the Fabruzzi family acquired it. In the 16th century it was handed over to the Church and, between 1751 and 1796, it was used by the Curia as a prison.

Notes

(1) *The reasons why so many towers were erected are still unclear, however many believe that, during the period of struggle for the pro-Emperor and pro-Pope investitures, the richest families used them as an offensive and/or defensive instrument, and <u>as a symbol of power</u>.*

In 1751, when the seminary of Bishop Paleotti, that comprised the tower and the adjoining house, was moved in front of the Chiesa di San Pietro, the tower was transformed into the Curia's male prison, a place of punishment for those who had committed crimes against religion, and had offended Christian morality. These crimes were expiated with bread and water, in poor hygienic conditions, and the threat to be transferred to the papal prisons (which were possibly even worse ?). The tower still shows some greatly suggestive signs of that gloomy period.

On the walls of the three cells (placed on the intermediate floors) several inscriptions cut by the prisoners are present, among which there is the inscription of a certain Angelo Rizzoli *"imprisoned for making two sisters pregnant"*, as he himself wrote. However, an even odder thing is that these inscriptions were executed using fragments of bricks or a mix consisting of brick powder and… body fluid.

On the right side of the standing tower, you will see another tower seemingly replicating, on a smaller scale, the two historic towers of Bologna (Asinelli and Garisenda), that is the

TORRE GUIDOZAGNI

UTILITY

 piazzetta S.Alò

 line n. 20, 28, A, B, BLQ (S.Pietro) 11, 27 (Indipendenza) 25, 29, 30, (Rizzoli)

It is another typical casatorre dating back to the beginning of the 13th century.

In 1487 it collapsed on the house below, and destroyed it. Consequently, the Bologna's Senate resolved to grant a contribution of 400 liras to Pietro Guidozagni, professor of Civil Law in the Bologna's "Studium", in order to enable the reconstruction of the tower.

Over the centuries it underwent several transfers of property until the beginning of the 20th century, when it was acquired by the Italian telephone company. Actually, this tower only managed to endure thanks to the timely intervention of the Fine Arts Department, that bound the company to carry out a "simple" rearrangement.

Walk back towards the Piazzetta S.Alò keeping the Torre Prendiparte on your right, continue straight towards the narrow road in front of you, Via Carbonara, take it and walk on straight until it comes out in Via del Monte, then turn left and, after a while, you will see the

UTILITY

via del Monte,8

line n. 11, 27, A, B (Indipendenza)

It was built in the first half of the 16th century according to a design by Jacopo Barozzi, an artist called "il Vignola", and was commissioned by the Boncompagni family (especially, by Ugo Boncompagni, who became Pope in 1572 taking the name of Gregory XIII and *promoted the Calendar Reform*).

The portal was the most important and precious element, but nowadays it is very damaged.

Inside visitors can admire sandstone

PALAZZO BONCOMPAGNI

columns and capitals attributed to Andrea Marchesi da Formigine, the capitals and the decorations are still well preserved.

The Boncompagni family is an Umbrian ancient aristocratic family. Rodolfo Boncompagni was appointed Lord of Assisi in 1133.

At the beginning of the 14th century the family moved to Bologna, where they made a name for themselves in economical and political fields to such an extent that one of their exponents became Pope. Actually, he was Cardinal Ugo Boncompagni, professor of law at the University of Bologna, who ascended the papal throne as Gregory XIII in 1572.

He was considered as one of the most important Popes in Modern Age, especially as regards to the implementation of the Catholic Reformation.

Pope Gregory XIII wanted that seminaries should be established everywhere, with the purpose of training the future priests, who had to be learned, morally irreproachable, and able to assume tasks related to religious renovation, as suggested by the Council of Trent.

Walk back into Via Carbonara and turn left, at the end of this road the palace you will see in front of you is the

PALAZZO BOCCHI

via Goito, 16

line n. 11, 27, A, B (Indipendenza)

UTILITY

It was erected between 1545 and 1560 for want of Achille Bocchi, who was known for being a learned philosopher. He transformed the tower into the seat of the Accademia Ermatena, founded by him.

The palace was designed by Vignola, assisted by Nocchi himself, and represents a beautiful example of Italian classical architecture.

At the base there are carvings containing lines by Horace in Latin, and some extracts from the Bible in Hebrew.

On the ground floor, inside a hall once used as seat of the Accademia Ermatena, a painting by Bartolomeo Cesi, *"Gods of Olympus"*, is housed, while the works by Prospero Fontana (disciple of Pierin de Vaga, through whom he was influenced by Raphael, Michelangelo and Tibaldi) still preserved are the frescoes on the vault and a *"Hercules"* above a chimney.

Achille Bocchi was a famous scholar of the Bologna's "Studio". In 1508, when he was only twenty years old, the University of Bologna gave him the chair of Greek Letters, then the chair of Rhetoric, followed by the chair of Poetics and, from 1525 onwards, the chair of Humanity.

On the base of the building he commissioned for himself, he had an inscription in Hebrew placed, which was extracted from Psalm 120 and has the following meaning: "O Lord, keep me from lying lips and deceiving language". Next to it, there is an inscription in Latin extracted from the first Epistle of Horace, which has the following meaning "They say you will be king if you act righteously".

Take the narrow road running beside the Palazzo Bocchi keeping the palace on your left, at the end of the road in front of you you will see the

PALAZZO GRASSI

🚏 **via Marsala, 12 ;** seat of the Officers' Club;
☎ +39.051.238183 🚌 line n. B, C (P.S.Martino) 11, 27, A (Indipendenza)

UTILITY

The palace dates back to the 13th century. However, between 1910 and 1913 it underwent renovation work that partially preserved the wooden portico.

Inside, there is a <u>gallery</u> decorated with stucco works by Carlo Nessi and a <u>chapel</u> with *"Mary Immaculate and angels"*, an artwork executed by the sculptor G. M. Mazza in 1706, with pictorial decorations by E. Graziani.

Inside a hall, within stucco frames, visitors can admire 17th century tempera paintings with perspectives by Andrea Monticelli.

A CURIOUS NOTE

The Grassi or de' Grassi aristocratic family is supposed to have Polish origins. In far-off times, they settled in Bologna, where they made a name for themselves and managed to become part of the senatorial order.

Among their exponents there were many Podestà (city's governors), Elders, Senators, Ambassadors and several Cardinals.

69

CHIESA DI SAN MARTINO MAGGIORE

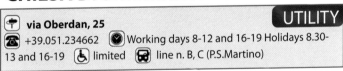

via Oberdan, 25
+39.051.234662 · Working days 8-12 and 16-19 Holidays 8.30-13 and 16-19 · limited · line n. B, C (P.S.Martino)

UTILITY

The church, also known as Madonna del Carmine, was built on an existing one and was enlarged towards the middle of the 15th century. From the first years of the 16th century onwards, it underwent some interventions that gave it its current appearance.

The lunette of the side portal facing Via Marsala features a terracotta high relief on a blue background, representing *"Saint Martin covering a poor man"*, a work by Francesco Mancini.

The façade was reinforced in the second half of the 17th century, to remedy the precarious static conditions of the bay that was built on the stream.

The Romanesque-Gothic bell tower was restored in 1728.

The façade, in Neo-Romanesque style, was rebuilt in 1879 according to a design by Giuseppe Modonesi, who added the mosaics and replaced the 16th century prothyrum with the current one.

A large circular window, having an ogival single-lancet window on either side, opens above the marble cusp-shaped prothyrum preceding the portal with mosaic lunette, which represents the preaching of Saint Martin.

Standing at the crossing between Via Marsala and Via Mentana, visitors can see the ancient apse, renovated in 1929 with the inclusion of copings, pinnacles and terracotta elements, and the bell tower.

<u>The interior</u> has three naves, while the perimeter chapels are divided by polygonal columns having low capitals with hook-shaped leaves. On these sit the ogival arches of the cross vaults featuring painted ribs. Three

square apses, covered with cross vaults, end the longitudinal development of the building. At the back of the right nave there is the chapel realized by Alfonso Torreggiani in 1753. In the church visitors can admire *fragments of frescoes* by Vitale da Bologna (14th century) and Paolo Uccello of the 15th century, a carved wooden *pulpit* dating back to 1724, *the organ* going back to 1624 and *works* by Jacopo della Quercia dating back to the end of the 14th century, Bartolomeo Cesi dating back to the 16th century, Francesco Francia dating back to the end of the 15th century, Ludovico Carracci dating back to the end of the 16th century, Girolamo da Carpi and Amico Aspertini dating back to the 16th century, and other.

Walk back to Via Oberdan and turn right, continue straight until you reach the crossing with Via A.Righi, there turn left and walk ahead until you reach Via Indipendenza (2nd crossing), where you will see the

BI-05
MP3

LUOGO DATO AGLI SPETTACOLI DIURNI

ARENA DEL SOLE

UTILITY

📍 **Via dell'Indipendenza, 44**
☎ +39.051.2910910   www.arenadelsole.it
🚌 line n. 11, 20, 27, 28, A (VIII Agosto) BLQ Aerobus (Arena del Sole), B, C (Righi)   ♿ good

It was built in masonry as outdoor theatre and inaugurated on July 5th 1810. Its architecture was neoclassical inspired.

Important companies and great actors performed in the Arena, among whom were Eleonora Duse, Irma Gramatica, Ermete Zacconi, Ermete Novelli, Ruggero Ruggeri, Dina Galli, Virginia Marini, Lyda Borelli, Ettore Petrolini, Maria Melato, Paola Borboni, Marta Abba and Renzo Ricci.

In 1984 the Municipality of Bologna purchased the building and in 1986 its radical renovation started, which led to the creation of the "Nuova Sede Teatro Stabile di Bologna" (New Seat of the Bologna's Permanent Theatre).

A CURIOUS NOTE

It was erected on the area of a Dominican convent that had been abandoned after the suppression of Religious Orders imposed by Napoleon Bonaparte (1796) who, after having declared the papal authority as forfeited, gave Bologna back the essence of its ancient government.

Continue straight along Via Indipendenza, pass the second crossing and, after a while, you will find the

CHIESA DI SAN BENEDETTO

UTILITY

 via Indipendenza, 64

 +39.051.247340

🕐 7.30-11 and 16-18.30 in August
the Church is open only for a few
hours during the morning;

🚌 line n. 11, 17, 27, 36, 37, 92, 95,
97, 98, A, B (VIII Agosto)

 limited

It has 13th century origins, although it was completely rebuilt in 1606 according to a design by G. B. Ballerini. The façade once faced Via Galliera, then it was renovated in 1892 with the addition of the portico, so as to adapt the church to the lay-out of the new Via dell'Indipendenza.

Inside visitors can admire *paintings* by G. Cavedoni, A. Tiarini, C. Aretusi, L. Massari, E. Procaccini il Vecchio, U. Gandolfi (1769) and a *statue* by A. G. Piò.

Walk straight along Via Indipendenza and, when this road ends, you will find in front of you an imposing construction, namely the

PORTA GALLIERA

UTILITY

📍 **Viale Masini**

🚌 line n. 32, 33, 38, 39
(p.ta Galliera)

♿ good

Like the other doors of Bologna, it had an important social and economical function since through it pedestrians and commercial wagons, coming from the area of

Galliera, entered the city across drawbridges.

Next to the door there was also the station for the payment of duties (tolls). This door was built in 1661 on the remains of that erected in the 13th century that was ruined. The architect Bartolomeo Provaglia gave it a typically Baroque appearance.

After passing Via Indipendenza you will reach the bus station square and, on your right, you will see the ruins of the ancient "Rocca di Galliera", belonging to the Pontifical Legation of Bologna and no longer showing the original medieval appearance.

A CURIOUS NOTE

Near the walls the ruins of which can still be seen, in the current Montagnola small hill, in the 14th century the Papal Legate Bertrando del Poggetto had a extremely magnificent fortress built.

The not-so-hidden objective was to create a symbol of the papal majesty (Bologna as Capital), to promote the return to Italy of the Pope, who had moved to Avignon (France) following the decisions of Clement V at the beginning of the century.

The economic oppression due to tax increase suffered by Bologna's citizens for want of the Papal Legate, the placing of highly recommended Frenchmen in the most important offices of political power, the intention of changing the City's Statutes, resulted all in a violent riot that led to the complete destruction of the fortress, of which nothing has remained today.

LA STAZIONE

 P.le Medaglie d'Oro

 UTILITY

 good

 line n. 21, 25, 30, 32, 33, 35, 36, 38, 39, 81, 87, 89, 91, 92, 93, 94, 95, A, C, D, BLQ (stazione Centrale)

This is the fifth Italian railway station as for dimension and traffic volume. It was built in 1851, but due to increase in traffic produced by its strategic position, twenty years later a new one was built in the current ancient position, which at that time was on the city outskirts. However, the

enlargement of the city caused the Central Railway Station to be located in the city centre and in the other economic entities.

Thanks to its importance as national crossing point towards all directions, it has been included in the so-called "High-Speed Trains" (TAV) plan, which envisages the use of trains operating at 300 km/h. For this purpose and exclusive use, an underground station is being constructed 23 metres under the actual surface, it will be 642 metres long and 56 metres wide.

On August 2nd, 1980, the station was the target of one of the most bloody terrorist act in the post-war period in Italy.

A bomb exploded in the 1st Class waiting room, 85 persons were killed and more than 200 were injured, some even seriously.

The part of the building destroyed was rebuilt, however, as you can see, the external wall was only plain plastered and painted a different colour to the rest of the building.

The watch was stopped at 10:25, time of the explosion, in order to keep alive the memory of this tragic event.

The breach opened in the wall of the waiting room was covered with glass, while a commemorative plaque nearby contains the names of the dead.

A CURIOUS NOTE

The first "Central Managers Team" in Italy was created in Bologna. On April 10th 1927 they started to manage the traffic of Porrettana line. The position of Central Manager originated in the United States. Towards the end of the 19th century, an officer of a Railway Company is said to have intervened by telegraph to settle the continuous disputes between the Station-masters, who did not agree on traffic management.

This idea was the beginning of the centralized control of train movements, thanks to which the managers knew all the information about the position of each running train.

The first Italian experiment of centralized management of train circulation started in 1927 on the Porrettana line, which was at that time one of the busiest Apennine passes.

On March 3rd 1927, the first Central Managers Team was established in Bologna. This event is recalled by a little picture containing the faces and the names of those forerunners, which is cherished in the office of the Head of Circulation Management Department of Bologna.

Walk back to the Porta di Galliera, then cross Via Indipendenza and go up the flight of steps leading to the

BI-01
MP3

PARCO DELLA MONTAGNOLA

It was realized in 1893 over a small hill created with filling material.

Initially it represented one of the magnificent parks of Bologna, where some fountains were also installed.

Then, for many years, it did not have a good reputation due to the disreputable people frequenting the park and the presence of drug traffic.

Now some structures have been created to make it enjoyable, and it seems to have attracted again the public that attended before.

At the foot of the flight of steps leading to Piazza VIII Agosto a sculptural group by Diego Sarti has been placed, which represents a horse and a woman figure attacked by an octopus.

Walk through the park along its walkways, until you reach the opposite exit to the

PIAZZA VIII AGOSTO

🪧 **Via Irnerio**

🚌 line n. 20, 28, 36, 37, 89, 93 94, 99 (Sferisterio)

UTILITY

The monument commemorates the expulsion of the Austrians by Bologna's citizens, occurred on August 8th 1848, and was inaugurated at the Montagnola on September 20th 1945, anniversary of the capture of Rome. It represents a Bologna's citizen raising the flag over the bodies of the adversaries.

Consulting the Thematic Library of Sala Borsa, you can learn that the inauguration had been fixed for the morning of August 8th and great publicity was given to the event. However, it was known that the demonstration would also be attended by the Catholic Associations, which had not been invited. Then, to protest against their presence, the Socialist Union organized a counterdemonstration to be held in the afternoon of that same day, to which also the workers associations adhered.

To prevent disorders from occurring, the City Council asked the Organizing committee to postpone the inauguration to September 20th, and they satisfied the request.

The square had always been the place assigned to the itinerant market, while all around it there were wholesalers' shops. After the construction of Centergross, the wholesalers moved their seats there, thus modifying the appearance of the square. It was dismantled to create a very large underground parking area, able to contain about 600 cars, that was inaugurated in December 2000.

When the square was rebuilt, the surface was transformed into a pedestrian area, where two days a week a traditional itinerant market, called "la Piazzola", takes place. This is frequented by Bologna's people, who are used to going shopping there.

"August 8th 1848 against the Austrians", this last battle seems to have originated from an accident (an Austrian officer had been mistreated in an eating house), and the Austrian army took this opportunity to enter the city.

Many members of the lower classes participated in the uprising, among them there were the porters of Via del Borgo di San Pietro and roughly armed citizens. The heart of the battle was the Montagnola and the square in front of it, which afterwards was called Piazza VIII Agosto. The Austrians lost more than four hundred men, while Bologna's people only lost about sixty men. Bologna was awarded the Medal as Well-deserving City of National Risorgimento.

Put your back to the monument and take Via Irnerio on your left, walk on until you reach Via Mascarella (5th crossing), where on your right you will see the

CHIESA DI SANTA MARIA E SAN DOMENICO DELLA MASCARELLA

It was built in the 18th century, but it was completely destroyed by the bombings in 1944. It was rebuilt during the post-war period, and paintings by T. Passarotti, B. Passarotti, Bagnacavallo, F. Torelli were placed back inside. On the first floor at number 44, there is the Oratorio di Santa Maria Maddalena, designed by

Alfonso Torreggiani in 1765, with paintings by G. M. and L. Crespi.

A CURIOUS NOTE

Some Spanish historians assert that the Collegiate Church of Roncesvalles obtained S. Maria della Mascarella (whether by acquiring it or by receiving it as a donation), that certainly already existed at the end of the 12th century, in order to use it as a dwelling for the canons who came to study in Bologna and, more generally, for the Spanish students attending the Bologna's Studio, and not as a "hospice" for pilgrims.

Tamburri came to this conclusion because, when in 1218 Saint Domenic came for the first time to Bologna with three or four companions, among whom there was one from Navarre, he turned to the Mascarella church and hospice.

Walk back along Via Mascarella and, at the end of this road, you will reach Via Belle Arti, where the palace on the right corner is the

PALAZZO DEI BENTIVOGLIO

📍 **Via Belle Arti, 8**
🕐 1st and 2nd Monday of each month (except the 1st Monday of January and August) from 8.30 to 10.30, the access is only limited to the two main halls, the oval hall, and the kitchen ♿ limited
🚌 line n. 20, 28, 36, 37, 89, 93, 94, 99 (p.ta S.Donato; Irnerio)

`UTILITY`

The current palace is not the first one that was built by this family, who governed the city between 1440 and 1500. In this period the city reaches an unequalled level of magnificence: art, science and the Studio assumed a primary role, and the consequent economic impulse positively affected the society. Churches, palaces and monuments were erected, while at that period the Bologna's Seigniory could rival the Sforza and Medici Seigniories. The situation changed firstly due to the unlucky influence of Cesare Borgia, and then to the taking of the city by Pope Julius II. The old palace, a beautiful building made of terracotta, was destroyed by popular fury in the spring of 1507. Later, in the 17th century, the Bentivoglio family erected a new palace that, although not as important as the former one, stands as evidence of Bologna's senatorial residence.

Besides the façade, the internal courtyard with double open gallery is also remarkable. It dates back to 1620 and is attributed to Falcetti, moreover it features unfinished decorations.

A CURIOUS NOTE

It seems that the happiest period of this family, affected by tragic events, was the Bologna's Renaissance. As for the origin of their name, legend tells about a love affair between Lucia, a countrywoman, and King Enzo, son of the Emperor Frederick II and prisoner of Bologna's citizens. He always repeated to her "ben-ti-voglio" ("I love you"), and their son was named after it. Actually, he is said to be the legendary founder of this family.

Keep the Palazzo Bentivoglio on your left and walk ahead along Via Belle Arti where, almost at the end of this road, on your left you will see the

PINACOTECA NAZIONALE

📍 **Via Belle Arti, 56**   `UTILITY`
☎ +39.051.4209411
🕐 Tuesday-Sunday 9-19, Closed: Monday, May 1st and August 16th;
♿ good
🚌 line n. 20, 28, 36, 37, 89, 93, 94, 99 (p.ta S.Donato)

It is located in ancient buildings used for Jesuit novitiate, and contains collections of artworks considered among the most important in Europe. Most of the works exhibited belong to Francesco and Giacomo Zambeccari and come from churches and convents that were closed during the Napoleonic domination. In 1815, after Napoleon's fall, these works returned to Italy.

Among others, here are displayed 14th century artworks by Vitale da Bologna, Pseudo Jacopino, a Bologna's painter operating between 1320 and 1330, Giotto and Lorenzo Veneziano, as well as Renaissance paintings, which include a "*Saint Cecilia*" by Raffaello and works by Perugino. Moreover, the Gallery has also rooms dedicated to the Baroque section with artworks by the Carraccis, Guido Reni, Guercino and other important masters.

After exiting the Pinacoteca take the narrow road in front of you that ends at Via Zamboni, then turn right, here the building you will see on your left is the

BI-02
MP3

PALAZZO POGGI – UNIVERSITA' DI BOLOGNA

🚏 via Zamboni, 33

UTILITY

Musei Palazzo Poggi: ☎ +39.051.2099398 🕙 Tue-Fri 10-13 and 14-16, Saturday and holidays 10.30-13.30 and 14.30-17.30, Closed: Monday; ℹ free (except during special events);

Museo della Specola: ☎ +39.051.2099360 🕙 Tue-Fri 0-13 and 14-16, Saturday and holidays: 10.30-13.30 and 14.30-17.30, Guided tours: Tue-Fri 10.30, 11.45, 14.30. Saturday and holidays: 11, 12.15, 15, 16.15. Visits for groups: by reservation; Closed: Monday, November 1st, December 8th, 24th, 25th, 26th, 31st, January 1st, Easter, April 25th, May 1st, June 2nd ℹ free

🚌 line n. 20, 28, 36, 37, 89, 93, 94, 99 (p.ta S. Donato) B (piazza Puntoni)

It houses the main seat of the University of Bologna and, from 1803, the rector's office.

It was built in the middle of the 16th century as dwelling of Alessandro Poggi and his brother, Cardinal Giovanni. The author of the design is a much debated question, some attributed it to Pellegrino Tibaldi, while others think it was realized by Bartolomeo Triachini. The interior is decorated with frescoes by Pellegrino Tibaldi.

On the ground floor there is the *"Aula Carducci"*,

dedicated to the poet who hold there lessons of Italian language and literature for 40 years; and the *"Sala dell'Ercole"*, that houses the statue representing the mythological hero sculpted by Angelo Piò in 1730.

The *Torre della Specola* was erected between 1712 and 1725, when the Palace became the seat of the Institute of Science.

In the Palace there are also several University Museums, while the rector's office and the Bologna's University Library hold the *Quadreria* consisting of more than 600 precious artworks. This iconographic collection was started in 1754.

The monumental *"Aula Magna"* (i.e., Lecture Theatre) situated along the northern side of the Palace, was inaugurated in 1756.

A CURIOUS NOTE

The origins of the "Studium" are owed to the gathering of eminent scholars of law called "glossarists", who were entrusted to comment upon the ancient Codes of Roman Law. Therefore, the first studies focused on the law, and among the first documented scholars are Pepone, Irnerio and Graziano (author of Concordantia discordantium canonum, namely the first manual of canon law).

In 1158 Frederick I promulgated the Costitutio Habita (or Authentica Habita), through which the University was safeguarded as place of research and study independent from any other power.

Walk back along Via Zamboni, the building you will find at number 34 is the

PALAZZO GOTTI

UTILITY

📍 **via Zamboni, 34**

🚌 line n. B (piazza Puntoni) C (Teatro Comunale)

This building was erected by the Fongarini family and, in 1780, was sold to the notary Pio Gotti. In 1791 it was completely transformed by Angelo Venturosi, to whom the façade, the entrance hall and the monumental staircase are attributed. The staircase is decorated with terracotta sculptures by Bonaventura Furlani.

A CURIOUS NOTE

Until the end of the 18th century, one of the mainstays of Bologna's economy was the art of silk weaving.

The quality standard reached and the refinement of the products created in the city occasioned a large export towards all Europe.

The famous "Bologna's voiles" determined the fortune of various families, among which was the Fongarini familiy.

This family too owned a "filatoglio alla bolognese", namely the Bologna's silk mill.

This advanced machine was fed by channels that today are almost all filled in, and which Bologna has plenty of. It was also protected against industrial espionage of that time, and its mechanisms were jealously guarded.

The punishments for those who tried to infringe the technological secrecy were especially severe, and this allowed the city to benefit from a long period of monopoly on the product.

The opposite road is Via Trombetti, and the building on your left is the

CA' GRANDE DEI MALVEZZI

Via Trombetti, 4
line n. B, C (Teatro Comunale)

UTILITY

It was built in 1444, enlarged during the following centuries and modernised in the 18th century for want of Sigismondo II Malvezzi.

Inside there are two halls frescoed by Ubaldo Gandolfi and Davide with "Hercules at crossroads" and "Hercules taken up to Olympus", bak to 1780; the ceilings with allegories were executed by Filippo ni and Davide Zanotti, while the "ancient-style" gallery was designed arlo Bianconi.

The Malvezzi family belonged to the Bologna's rich landed aristocracy. Originally they came from Budrio (a town of the current province), and were also prominent figures of Bologna's political life and occupied several public offices from 1466 up to 1797.

The silk commerce and the development of bank activities enabled the family to accumulate vast wealth.

The large halls of the palace became famous thanks to the important historical figures who frequented them, and the great parties and weddings that were celebrated there, among which there were the famous weddings between Giulio Malvezzi and Camilla Sforza, and between Piriteo Malvezzi and Beatrice Orsini.

When Piriteo died (1806) the family came to an end, and in 1827 the palace was acquired by the Pontifical University. Today it is part of the buildings belonging to the University of Bologna.

Walk back to Via Zamboni, turn left and the building you will see on your left is the

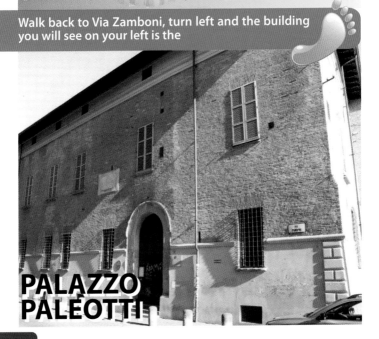

PALAZZO PALEOTTI

> ⬆ **via Zamboni, 25**
> 🚌 line n. 14, 19, 25, 27 (S.Vitale) C (Teatro Comunale)

UTILITY

It was built by the Salaroli family towards the end of the 15th century, and still keeps the beautiful courtyard dating back to that epoch and decorated with 16th century frescoes.

On the noble floor are housed friezes by Domenico degli Ambrogi and Girolamo Curti (called il Dentone) going back to around 1620.

Currently it is at the disposal of the University of Bologna.

A CURIOUS NOTE

Andrea Paleotti, a Bologna's noble, became very famous in 1650, when he was almost thirty four years old, because he married Cristina Dudley of Northumberland dukes, who was not even thirteen years old. Bologna's citizens gave the child bride a very enthusiastic welcome. In the August of that year she gave birth a baby girl, but it was rumoured that, before marrying, she had had a daughter from Prince Lorenzo Onofrio Colonna, High Constable of the Kingdom of Naples, and this could explain the reason why she was betrothed to as a "seedy" noble as Paleotti.

Cristina Paleotti was not only beautiful, but she was also remembered as the protagonist of several scandals, although she continued to live with her husband inside the Bologna's beautiful palace in the former Via San Donato, that today is Via Zamboni. During those years, the beautiful, intelligent and likeable lady passed from one rich lover to another, thus becoming the cause for various duels not only in Bologna.

She was a resourceful woman, and when she lost a diamond jewel, did not get discouraged and promised a considerable reward in case of restitution.

The jewel was never found again, but the marchesa received an even more precious jewel from Count Ercole Pepoli, with whom she had a short romance.

Right in front there is the

BI-03
MP3

TEATRO COMUNALE

> ⬆ **Largo Respighi, 1**
> ☎ +39.051.529011 🕐 Tue-Fri 15-19 Saturday 10-12.30 and 15-19 ♿ good 🚌 line 14, 19, 25, 27 (S.Vitale), C (Teatro Comunale)

UTILITY

This 18th century building represents one of the main centres of the Italian opera, and it is also the Italian second most ancient theatre after the San Carlo Theatre in Naples. It can accommodate 1.200 spectators.

The acoustics of the theatre is excellent and allows the audience to fully enjoy the performances taking place there, which also include, besides operas, symphony and chamber concerts.

The theatre has a symphony orchestra and a choir well-known for its tradition and quality.

The Bologna's Teatro Comunale was built by Antonio Galli da Bibbiena in the spot where once there was the Bentivoglio's Domus Aurea, that was destroyed in 1507. Part of the remains constitute the current Giardini del Guasto (which once was part of the large and sumptuous palace of Bentivoglio family, that ruled Bologna until 1506. The following year this palace was completely destroyed by popular fury).

The Bentivoglio's Guasto remained abandoned until the middle of the 18th century, when the Teatro Comunale was erected on most of the area.

continue walking along Via Zamboni, and the building you will see on your left is the

BI-04-1
MP3

BI-04-2
MP3

CHIEDA DI SAN GIACOMO MAGGIORE

UTILITY

📍 **Piazza Rossini**

☎ +39.051.225970

🕐 Mon-Fri 7.30-13 and 15.30-18.30; Sat-Sun 8.30-13 and 15.30-18.30 ♿ very limited

Oratorio S.Cecilia: 🕐 see the list of oratories. During the church services, the sightseeing could be limited or suspended.

🚌 line 14, 19, 25, 27 (S.Vitale), C (Teatro Comunale)

It was built by Augustinian monks starting from 1267. *The apse* and the *radial chapels* date back to 1331-43; *the bell tower* dates back to 1336-1472; the *portico* dates back to 1477-81; the *chapels and the vaults of the nave* date back to 1493-99. It houses several artworks, which include *paintings* by P. Veneziano, Jacopo di Paolo, Simone de' Crocifissi, P. Fontana, E. Procaccini, B. Passarotti, Innocenzo da Imola and L. Carracci. During the Seigniory of Bentivoglio family, whose palace stood nearby, the church and the convent were really important for the city. The suppression of Religious Orders, following the French occupation, caused the destination of

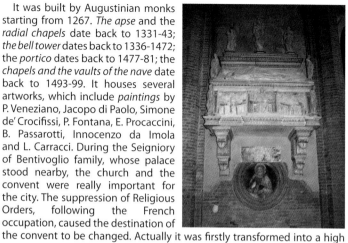

the convent to be changed. Actually it was firstly transformed into a high school specializing in music education, and then into a "Musical Conservatory", that had among its professors some distinguished composers such as Gioacchino Rossini, Gaetano Donizetti and Ottorino Respighi. Behind the church there is the Oratorio di S.Cecilia. It houses *ten paintings* by important artists of that time, which represent, in a sequence, the life of the patron Saint of musicians.

A CURIOUS NOTE

The *Eremitani* (Augustinians), who followed the rule of Saint Augustine, started to erect their building towards 1267. However, the continuous contrasts between a part of the clergy and the Ghibelline factions caused the works to proceed slowly. It was only after 1282, when the popular-oriented and religion-supporter Guelph faction became stronger, that the works started to progress regularly again, also thanks to the several and massive financial supports that the Bologna's Senate and the people destined to the construction of the building, through both direct donations and the collection of the gabelle (tolls) at the doors of S. Donato and S. Vitale.

The first donation was decided on April 27th 1285, when the People's Captain was Corso Donati, who is also mentioned in Dante's Divine Comedy (Purg. XXIV, 82-90).

After exiting the church, you will be in Piazza Rossini and the palace you will see on your right is the

PALAZZO MAGNANI-SALEM

via Zamboni, 20

line n. 14, 19, 25, 27 (S.Vitale) B, C (Teatro Comunale)

good

The construction was entrusted to Domenico Tibaldi by Lorenzo Magnani, and it dates back to about the end of the 16th century.

On the noble floor there is the famous cycle of frescoes by Ludovico, Annibale and Agostino Carracci, representing the "Stories of Rome's foundation"; the monumental chimney was realized by Floriano Ambrosiani, and it is decorated with statues by Gabriele Fiorini, who is also the author of the "Hercules" in the courtyard and the "bust of Lorenzo Magnani" on the hall's door.

Put your back to the church, and look at the opposite palace having its main entrance in Via Zamboni, that is the

PALAZZO MALVEZZI

UTILITY

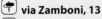 **via Zamboni, 13**

☎ +39.051.6598218 ⏰ it can be only visited on the occasion of special events 🚌 line n. 14, 19, 25, 27 (S.Vitale) C (Teatro Comunale)

92

The building was erected for want of Paola Malvezzi on the spot where a pre-existing family palace stood, and in a part of the churchyard bought from the friars of San Giacomo Maggiore.

The design was entrusted to Bartolomeo Trachini, who realized it in 1560. In 1725 it underwent the first modifications with the *important monumental staircase* executed by Alfonso Torregiani, according to a design by Ferdinando Bibiena, and then modified around 1930.

During the years 1852-53, Giovanni Malvezzi de' Medici ordered a rearrangement of the rooms, and the works were entrusted to a group of Bologna's artists and artisans: the decorative techniques used enabled the frescoes to be well-preserved.

On the noble floor there are 19th century decorations by F. Cocchi, A. Muzzi, G. Dal Pane, G. Badiali, A. Pesci, L. Samoggia (1852-53).

The Malvezzi family lived in the palace until 1930, when it was bought by Bologna's provincial administration.

Continue walking along Via Zamboni, turn right to the first narrow road, there you will reach one of the entrance to the

IL GHETTO

The major road of the ghetto was Via dell'Inferno, to which a braid of narrow roads came together. Today they are called Via dei Giudei, Via Canonica, Vicolo di San Giobbe, Vicolo Mandria, Via del Carro and Via Valdonica.

This is a large area that was closed by two gates: the first one stood at the entrance to Via dei Giudei, while the second one stood in the today's Via Oberdan, in the large arch leading to Vicolo Mandria through the current Vicolo Tubertini.

The Synagogue was in Via dell'Inferno, at number 16. Nowadays a memorial slab has been located on the building.

The ghetto is exactly in the city's medieval centre, and it still holds its original urbanistic structure. The whole area features those same gloomy zones, narrow hallways and courtyards where the Bologna's Hebrews were confined by the State of the Church from the year 1556.

They were expelled in 1569 and, after many vicissitudes, definitively driven out in 1593. They were about 900 persons, and for more than two centuries no organized Jewish group was allowed to live in the city.

The 15th century Bologna's Hebrews animated an important centre of Jewish studies, thanks to the presence of learned rabbis and printing houses where sacred books were printed.

From 1525 Ovadià Sforno[1] run a school of Talmudic studies[2] in the city, while Azzarià de' Rossi, one of the main scholars of the 16th century, stayed for long time in Bologna.

In 1488 a chair of Hebraism was established in the city's University.

Notes

[1] He was born in Cesena in 1470, and was Rabi, doctor, philosopher and a commentator of Jewish legalism. He was a great figure of the medieval Italian Judaism.

[2] The Talmud is one of the sacred text of Judaism. It means teaching or study.

It was Pope Paul IV Carafa (important inquisitor) who issued the bull *"Cum nimis absurdum"* in 1555.

In all the territories subject to Church's temporal power, the Hebrews were separated from the rest of people.

The rules were precise, below are some examples:

- … if the number of Hebrews was limited, they had to live in the same house (*the Hebrew's house*).

- … if the number of Hebrews did not allow them to live in the same house, they had to live in the same road (*the giudecca*).

- … if even this was not possible, their area had to be surrounded by a walls with entrances and exits provided with gates (*the ghetto*), which were opened at sunrise and closed at sunset.

- … they could have only one Synagogue

- … men were obliged to wear a yellow hat (later it was red).

- … women were obliged to wear a yellow veil (like the prostitutes).

- … *they could only deal in second-hand clothes and old objects, or have a loan desk where the interest rate could not exceed 12%.*

After you reach Via dell'Inferno, turn left and walk ahead along the alleys until you come out in Via Oberdan. Now turn left and continue ahead until the end, namely Via Rizzoli, there turn right and, after a while, you will be in the starting point, which is the end of this tour.

TOUR

3

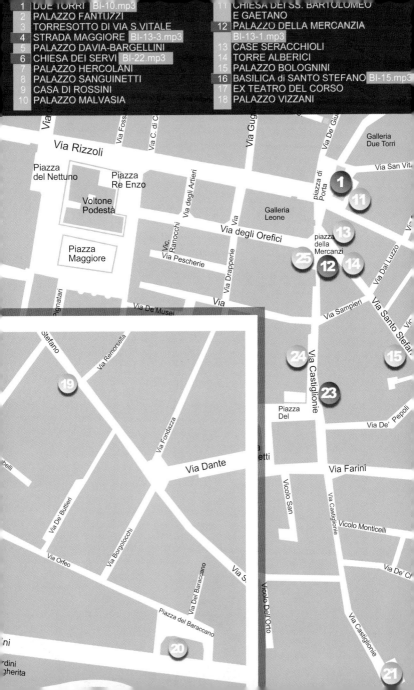

19 PALAZZO BOSDARI AGUCCHI
20 SANTUARIO DELLA MADONNA
   DEL BARACCANO
21 EX CHIESA DI SANTA LUCIA
22 CHIESA DI S.GIOVANNI IN MONTE
   OLIVETO
23 PALAZZO PEPOLI VECCHIO BI-13-2.mp3
24 PALAZZO PEPOLI CAMPOGRANDE
25 PALAZZO BOLOGNETTI

Tappe del percorso

Tappe del percorso
con Audioguida

Nome del file audio

This tour starts from the most traditional spot of the city, namely the

BI-10
MP3

DUE TORRI

📍 **Piazza di Porta Ravegnana**   UTILITY

Torre degli Asinelli: 🕐 Summer 9-18 (last ascent: 17.40), Winter 9-17 (last ascent: 16.40); **Torre Garisenda:** cannot be visited;

🚌 line n. 11, 13, 14, 19, 25, 27, 29, 30 (Rizzoli) A (P.Maggiore) B (S.Pietro)

They are "twin" towers, symbol of Bologna. These are built in masonry and do not correspond to the wooden original ones. They had a lookout and defensive function. The most striking ones of the 17 towers still preserved inside the walls are: The Torre Garisenda - It is the more ancient of the two Towers, and is likely to date back to the turn of the 12th century. The unsuitable ground on which it was erected (the torrent Aposa flows below) caused a settling when the tower reached the height of 60 metres, thus interrupting the initial ambitious design. Later it escaped from being demolished only because the Municipality was experiencing a deep financial crisis, and did not have the sums of money necessary to expropriate it from the Garisenda family. In 1350 the Giovanni Visconti da Oleggio, who then was Governor of Bologna, established a lowering of about 12 metres (m 48.16) for safety's reasons.

The Torre degli Asinelli - It was erected by the homonymous family between 1109 and 1119 with more "modern" building methods. It is 97.20 metres high, and it features a 2.23-meters steep drop and an internal staircase with 498 steps. During the 14th century the Municipality acquired the Tower, thus transforming it from an instrument of prestige and defence for the Asinelli family into a jail, as well as observation and signalling point over large distances thanks to its "lumiera" (a sort of lantern case) placed at the top. The base was added in 1488 and housed the guard soldiers. Over the years the Asinelli tower had been frequently struck by lightning due to its height, until when in 1824 the Professor of Physics Francesco Orioli was engaged in supervising the works for the installation of a lightning rod. The last dangers were the bombing of the Second World War. In that period the Asinelli tower was used as a sighting point to superintend the rescue work during and after the German air raids.

On September 25th 1943 a bomb just missed the two towers, struck and destroyed the houses placed on the corner between Via Zamboni and Via San Vitale. However, a great deal of luck allowed them to be preserved until now.

Along this tour you will have the opportunity to see other towers.

After walking around the towers and, if you want, going up the 498 steps for a staggering view, take the diagonal road at the back of the Garisenda tower, Via S.Vitale. Walk straight ahead along this road until, after the sixth side street, on your right you will see the

PALAZZO FANTUZZI

via San Vitale, 23

line n. 14, 19, 25, 27 (S.Vitale)

UTILITY

The façade was built in the 16th century according to a design attributed to Formigine, and it is marked by ashlar semi-columns. The decoration with elephants refers to the family's coat of arms.

Inside there is a monumental staircase designed by Paolo Canali in 1680 with statues by Gabriele Bunelli. On the noble floor there exists a representative hall with "*perspectives*" by Francesco Galli Bibiena dating back to 1684, and a hall with frescoes by A. M. Colonna.

A CURIOUS NOTE

In the 16th century, the oligarchic - republican system of city's government forced the distinguished senatorial families to erect palaces pointing out the rank and the power of the owners.

Also the important merchant Fantuzzi family, that belonged to the city's aristocracy, built its sumptuous dwelling.

In front of you, you will see the

TORRESOTTO DI VIA SAN VITALE

🚏 **via San Vitale, 56**
🚌 line n. 14, 19, 25, 27 (S. Vitale) C (P. Aldrovandi)

UTILITY

The *Torresotto*[1] or *Serraglio* (small tower) *di San Vitale* belongs to the second circle of the walls, which is actually called *Cerchia dei Torresotti* or, improperly, *del Mille*.

It stands between Via San Vitale and Piazza Aldrovandi, that is built on the area where in ancient times the moat run.

Note

[1] *Bologna was surrounded by three circles of walls. The second one was started in the late 12th century, and it was called Cerchia **dei Torresotti** due to the presence of fortified structures located close to the doors.*

A CURIOUS NOTE

The Bologna's economic boom during the previous centuries had attracted to the city many people, brought in by the hope of a better life, so the city's buildings had been erected far beyond the selenite walls of the first circle. Therefore, the need increased to extend safety to the new buildings as well, by incorporating them within new walls.

These new walls was surrounded by a moat fed by the torrent Aposa, and they had a circular lay-out, unlike the first circle that had a square lay-out.

Cross the Torresotto and turn right to Piazza Aldrovandi, then walk on until the end, where you will reach the

BI-13-3
MP3

STRADA MAGGIORE

line n. 14, 19, 25, 27 (str.Maggiore)

UTILITY

It is full of ancient noble palaces from all epochs, that are among the most interesting ones of the city.

You can admire magnificent façades, decorated portals and hidden gardens.

Also the Strada Maggiore is a city's section of the important Via Emilia, that connects Via Flaminia (Rimini) and Via Postumia (Piacenza). This major road was built by Romans in the 2nd century BC, to allow the armies to move rapidly so as to put down any uprisings around the Piacenza's colony.

At those times this colony was surrounded by Galli Boi, a partially defeated Gallic population that had not wanted to sign the peace with Rome. Today the Via Emilia is still the major road of Emilia-Romagna.

The palace standing on the corner on your left is the

UTILITY

📍 **Strada Maggiore,44 Museo Civico d'Arte industriale and Galleria Davia Bargellini:**

☎ +39.051.236708

🕐 Tue-Sat 9-14, Sunday and holidays 9-13, closed: Monday (if not holyday), January 1st, May 1st, December 25th;

ℹ free 🚌 line n. 14 19, 25, 27 (str. Maggiore) C (piazza Aldrovandi);

♿ good

PALAZZO DAVIA-BARGELLINI

It stands in Strada Maggiore in front of the Chiesa dei Servi, and it is one of the major buildings of Bologna.

The construction of the family's new aristocratic palace, on the spot already occupied by buildings owned by Bargellini family since 1610, was wanted by Camillo Bargellini that, in 1638, entrusted the design to Bartolomeo Provaglia, who was supported by the master builder Antonio Uri.

The architect worked out some solutions for the palace, that was erected within 1658, and renounced the classical structure with portico in order to point out its uniqueness and solemnity, in a space that was left open by the portico in front of the Basilica di Santa Maria dei Servi

This building represents the most important example of the 17th century architecture in Bologna, in which you can find the 16th century local brick curtain arrangement.

It has no portico and is organized on three levels divided by horizontal moulded bands, with windows marked by sandstone frames and surmounted by triangular and curvilinear pediments.

The central balcony is supported by two sandstone telamons realized by Gabriele Brunelli and Francesco Agnesini, which rest on ashlar pedestals. The two statues, called "giganti" ("*giants*"), made the building famous also with the name of "Palazzo dei Giganti" ("*Giants' Palace*").

The plain ashlar angle bars on the corners highlight and reinforce the shoe-type base of the palace.

The windows on the façade are surmounted by a tympanum on the ground floor, by a depressed arch on the first floor, and by a simple frame on the last floor.

<u>In the interior</u>, beside the central loggia on the ground floor, there is the baroque grand staircase with a majestic tenaille development, realized in the 18th century and attributed to Carlo Francesco Dotti.

<u>In the halls on the first floor</u> are housed artworks by important painters, such as Vitale da Bologna, Bartolomeo Vivarini, Innocenzo da Imola, Amico Aspertini, Bartolomeo Passerotti, Camillo Procaccini, Mastelletta, Giacomo Cavedoni, Luigi Crespi and others.

The palace was bequeathed to the Davia family, and in 1876 the marquis Giuseppe left this building and all his property to a Charitable Institution engaged in educating young people, that later was named Davia Bargellini.

Giuseppe Davia has also the merit to have started the collection of paintings that the Charitable Institution enlarged and diversified, adding furniture and equipment which had belonged to Bologna's middle-class and noble houses.

Today, paintings and objects form the possessions of the Gallery of the Opera Pia Davia Bargellini and the Museo Civico d'Arte Industriale, founded by Francesco Malaguzzi Valeri in 1924, which currently are both housed inside the Palace.

The halls used as museum are decorated with ornaments and particulars executed according the baroque taste, however they are realized in a measured way and in agreement with the sober character of the whole building.

The museum is characterized by the variety of pieces displayed, furniture, metal, glass and ceramic objects, fabrics, worked wooden pieces, although the collection is actually small.

We find the first traces of the Bargellini family in the second half of the 14th century, during which some of its exponents were registered as members of Craft Guilds. The following century was maybe the most significant one for this family, since several of its exponents occupied some of the most important administrative offices of city government. The last exponent having the right to the senatorial title, that over the centuries had been handed down among the family's various branches, was Bernardino Pasquale Innocenzo Melchiorre Lucio Bargellini, who succeeded his father in the senatorial seat in 1771, and he held it until the suppression of the Bologna's Senate in 1797.

Upon his death Bernardino Bargellini, who was unmarried and with no heirs, left a part of his property for the settlement of an annuity aimed at "maintaining and endowing young women and comforting sick beggars".

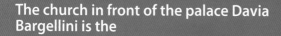

The church in front of the palace Davia Bargellini is the

BI-22
MP3

CHIESA DEI SERVI

Strada Maggiore, 4

UTILITY

Segreteria della Cappella Musicale di S. Maria dei Servi:
☎ +39.051.261710 ♿ good; 🚌 line n. 14, 19, 25, 27 (str.Maggiore)

This is an ancient basilica located at 43 Strada Maggiore, from which you can enjoy a splendid view over the portico.

The construction was started in 1345, it was enlarged by Andrea Manfredi in 1383 and finished by Andrea Faenza in the 16th century. The side portico is attributed to Antonio di Vincenzo, that made it in 1392 approximately. It was enlarged and renovated in the 17th century for the Servite order. It was completed between the end of the 18th century and the middle of the year 1855, thus assuming the current square appearance. The Basilica dei Servi, like the one of San Petronio, also expresses the culture of Bologna's late Gothic art,

namely an especially happy period. The church features a basilican layout with three naves. The vaults are supported by masonry pointed arches, which are typical of Gothic art. The apse also has a terracotta decoration. This church houses several artworks, among which visitors can admire the "Blessed Virgin and Child on the throne" by Cimabue, one of the most important artists of early Italian painting, the marble altarpiece representing the "Annunciation to Mary" by Michelangelo, traces of frescoes from the 14th century by Vitale da Bologna, a fresco by Guido Reni, the Four Angels, and numerous other paintings. The church is also the venue for classical music concerts always attended by a large audience. On December 13th a fair dedicated to Saint Lucy takes place under the portico, and here you can buy Christmas trees, the statues of the shepherds and other decorations for Christmas crib and tree, toys and Christmas sweets.

Ronzano.

From 1947 its director is Father Pellegrino Cantucci, whose first task was to reconstruct what the war had destroyed. After overcoming hesitations and mistrusts of his "superiors", he replaced the children (white voices) by women, mainly recruited in a convent of orphan girls. Now the Musical Chapel consists of eighty choristers divided into four different voice tones: Sopranos, Contraltos, Tenors, Bassos, who do not receive any kind of remuneration, but are driven by the sole desire of singing and being able to transmit a special type of music culture to the audience.

Walk on along the portico on the church's side until the end, then on your right you will see the

PALAZZO HERCOLANI

UTILITY

 Strada Maggiore, 45
 line n. 14, 19, 25, 27
(Torleone)

It was erected by the architect Angelo Venturoli from 1793 onwards, for the princely branch of Hercolani family. This palace was completed at the beginning of the 19th century.

In the design Venturoli recovered classical elements typical of the 16th century architectural tradition, such as in the façade. <u>The grand staircase</u> echoes the baroque taste; the loggia with stucco statues was executed in 1800 by Giacomo de Maria, while the vault above, representing the *"Apotheosis of Hercules"*, was realized by Master Filippo Pedrini. <u>On the ground floor</u>, inside a hall having curved walls announcing the marvellous winter garden, Rodolfo Fantuzzi painted the "Boschereccia" ("*Woodland*") in 1810.

<u>On the vault of the staircase</u> Filippo Pedrini and D. Zanotti painted the *"Glory of Hercules"* around 1799.

<u>On the noble floor</u> there is the honour hall (today called "Aula Ruffilli"),

with the *"Apollo and the Hours"*, embedded into a scenery animated by *harpies*, *genies*, *medallions* and *four busts* of poets, among which is *Dante*, an artwork dating back to 1798 and realized by Filippo Pedrini and F. Minozzi. Two halls were decorated by Vincenzo Armani and D. Zanotti in Chinese style. Several different artists contributed to the decoration of the *following halls*, among whom are L. Busatti, S. Barozzi, A. Basoli, P. Fancelli and G. Frulli. Currently the palace houses the Faculty of Political Science of the University of Bologna, that bought it from the Hercolani family in 1973.

A CURIOUS NOTE

The Hercolani family was a Bologna's ancient family.

It is well-known the relationship esisting during the 19th century between the illustrious musician Gioacchino Rossini and some exponents of this family.

There was such a great friendship that, when the young prince Astorre Hercolani was poorly off and asked Rossini for a considerable monetary loan, relying exclusively on his word, namely 140,000 liras (about half a million euros), he generously granted it to him. When Rossini was at death's door, in 1868, his second wife, Olimpia Pallissier, sent to Bologna their lawyers to require the repayment of the loan from the prince.

He was unable to honour it, so he mortgaged a part of the family's collection in favour of the Master.

This is how in 1883, after some judicial proceedings, the Municipality of Pesaro, i.e. the final beneficiary of Rossini's legacy, came into possession of the mortgaged paintings.

Walk back along Strada Maggiore towards the city's centre until you reach number 34, there on your right you will see the

PALAZZO SANGUINETTI
(formerly Aldini)

UTILITY
🪧 **Strada Maggiore, 34**
Museo Musicale:
☎ +39.051.2757711
🕐 Tue-Fri 9.30-16 Saturday and holidays 10-18.30, closed: Monday if not holiday, January 1st, May 1st, December 25th;
ℹ free
♿ good 🚌 line n. 14, 19, 25, 27 (str. Maggiore)

At the beginning of the 16th century it belonged to the noble Loiani family. In 1569 the palace was acquired by Riario brothers, and it was rebuilt and enlarged with a grand staircase that represents its distinguishing feature. The ancient façade was wanted by Cardinal Riario in the middle of the 16th century. In 1796, the palace was granted on emphyteusis to the lawyer count Antonio Aldini, who carried out an important structural intervention: in 1798 he engaged the architect G.B. Martinetti, who redesigned the façade by keeping the terracotta cornice with frieze and extending it along three arches of the portico. The main decorations date back to this same epoch: they still make this palace an extraordinary historical-artistic property, that is among the most important Italian monuments of neoclassicism.

On the background of the courtyard is a *perspective* by L. Busatti dating back to 19th century. Inside visitors can admire *paintings* by S. Barozzi, A. Basoli, P.Facelli, G. Lodi and the *"boschereccia-style"* hall by V. Martinelli and P. Palagi going back to 1805. After the ruin of the Aldini family, the palace was sold to the Cuban noble Pegnalverd, who in 1832 sold it to the tenor Domenico Donzelli. In 1870, it was acquired by the Sanguinetti family, to which the most recent decorations are owned. In 1986, they donated the palace to the Municipality of Bologna, in order to transform it to Musical Museum and Library.

A CURIOUS NOTE

The lawyer count Antonio Aldini was professor of law in the University of Bologna. He was entrusted with positions of responsibility in the Cisalpine Republic, the Italian Republic and the Italic Kingdom. The count was man of confidence of Napoleon Bonaparte in Bologna, and played a first-rate role during the revolutionary period that followed the arrival of the French, then he was also appointed Minister Secretary of State in the Kingdom of Italy.

After the failed conspiracy on November 14th 1794, that was aimed at giving Bologna back that independency lost due to the Papal State, the Jacobin leaders Luigi Zamboni (one of the first martyrs in the name of the republic and inventor of the Italian tricolour) and Giovanni Battista de Rolandis were arrested and tortured. Whilst Zamboni died in jail, Antonio Aldini undertook the defence of De Rolandis, in a desperate and useless attempt to save his life. The patriot from Asti was condemned to death and hanged in Bologna on April 27th 1796.

Continue walking along Strada Maggiore until you reach number 26 on the right, there you will find the

CASA DI ROSSINI

Strada Maggiore, 26

line n. 14, 19, 25, 27 (str. Maggiore)

UTILITY

Gioachino Rossini, one of the most important Italian composers, was born in Pesaro. His father was from Lugo and his mother from Urbino. Due to their political ideas, the family was forced to wander from town to town in Emilia Romagna, so Rossini spend his youth living with his grandmother or travelling to Ravenna, Ferrara and Bologna. He attended the Bologna's Musical Secondary School, and started to compose in this city.

In 1822 he married the opera singer Isabella Colibran, and in 1824 had his house in Bologna built, where he lived for a long period, until he emigrated to Paris, maybe because he was embittered and disappointed by envy (however, the actual reasons are still unknown).

A CURIOUS NOTE

On the façade of the house musical emblems and a Latin distich are cut. The distich says: *"Non domo dominus sed domino domus"* (it is not the owner who had to become proud of the house, but the house of the owner).

Continue walking along Strada Maggiore until you reach number 22 on the right, there you will find the

.AZZO MALVASIA

Strada Maggiore, 22

line n. 14, 19, 25, 27 (str. Maggiore)

UTILITY

It was handed over to the Malvasia family in 1535, and they charged Formigine to build the façade while preserving the 15th portico.

The elegant spiral staircase was realized by Gian Carlo Sicinio Bibiena in 1750 approximately, and was decorated with stucco statues representing *"Sisyphus"* and *"Minerva"*, executed by Filippo Scandellari.

Walk on along Strada Maggiore, and short before reaching the two towers you will find the

CHIESA DEI SS. BARTOLOMEO and GAETANO

UTILITY

🕆 **strada Maggiore, 4**

☎ +39.051.22.76.92;

🕙 working days 7.30-12.30 and 15.30-19 holidays 8.30-13 and 15.30-19;

♿ very limited

🚌 line n. 14, 19, 25, 27 (Rizzoli)

On the spot where the current basilica stands, in the 13th century there was a small church having the façade overlooking the Piazza di Porta Ravegnana. A pre-existent church dedicated to Saint Bartholomew seems to have been erected there. In 1516, the Gozzadini family entrusted a design to Andrea Marchesi (called il Formigine), which also included the renovation of the existing church. In 1516 the works were interrupted; in that moment only the portico had been realized, which is the current one. In 1627 the Theatine Fathers, who were governors of the church, started a complete renovation of the complex by entrusting the design to Giovanni Battista Natali (called il Falzetta). It was also examined by the architect of the Bologna's Senate, Agostino Borelli. A new larger building was erected, that incorporated the portico, while

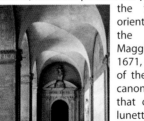

the façade was oriented towards the Strada Maggiore. In 1671, the founder of the Order of Theatines, Saint Cajetan, was canonized, and the Fathers joined his title to that of apostle Bartholomew. Therefore, the lunettes of the portico were decorated with scenes from the life of Saint Cajetan. The 15th century portal of the previous church, which is placed on the side overlooking the Two Towers, was kept, while in 1694 the bell tower and the dome were completed. The bell tower's spire was added half a century later.

PALAZZO DELLA MERCANZIA

 Piazza della Mercanzia, 4

UTILITY

☎ +39.051.6093111 ⓘ free 🚌 line n. 11, 13, 14, 19, 25, 27 (Rizzoli)

♿ limited

It was built in 1381 and used as seat of the Merchants' Guild, a body responsible for settling any disputes arising between buyers and sellers and having judicial functions. In case of commercial disputes, these were settled by a Judge, assisted by five merchants called Consuls. There was also a court of second instance with a Judge of Appeal, assisted by four Superconsuls. The Judges, Consuls and Superconsuls remained in charge for 6 months, and were appointed by drawing lots before the Elders and the Gonfalonier of Justice, in the presence of the pro tempore Judges and Consuls.

The statutes of the Guilds were drawn up and modified by the Statutieri (some sort of legislators), in the palace there were eight of them. They were elected every 5 years. Lastly, there was the Curator, a notary in charge of the Archive and the Chamber of the Deeds of the Notaries in the Court; this was a life office. Bologna can boast the right of primogeniture for this type of institution as well.

This palace features beautiful Gothic forms, while in its battlements the guilds' coats of arms are represented. In the two pointed arches of the arcade stands the statue of the Justice. Along the 19th century flight of steps there are the coats of arms of the judges of the Court.

The Palazzo della Mercanzia was built between 1384 and 1391 on a design by Antonio di Vincenzo (he was the architect of the Basilica di San Pietro) and Lorenzo da Bagnomarino. In that place the old Customhouse or Gabelle office stood. In 1888 it underwent a renovation carried out by Alfonso Rubbiani.

The cement anchorages you see in front of the palace bounded the area that once was occupied by the money changers' benches, actually a very profitable activity from time immemorial.

The 15th century memorial slab, which is written in Latin and is placed on the side of the Palazzo della Mercanzia overlooking Via Castiglione, recalls one of the strategies used by the Municipality of Bologna to make the city appealing to students: the right to free books, clothes and board.

Put your back to the two towers and, standing on the left side of the square, you will see the

CASE SERACCHIOLI

Piazza Mercanzia, 3

UTILITY

line n. 11, 13, 14, 19, 20, 25, 27, 29, 30 (Rizzoli) A (P.Maggiore)

In Piazza Mercanzia visitors can admire the beauty of the palace and some examples of medieval houses.

The house on the left is the Casa Seracchioli, that dates back to the 13th century and still keeps the door and the arched windows in the mezzanine. The modern brick façade refers to the Bologna's medieval models with lancet arched small windows.

Both the building on the left (Casa Seracchioli) and the one on the right (Casa Reggiani), the ancient balcony of which was fitted in 1924 over the wooden portico previously restored, were originally used as "Gabelle offices"

Take Via S.Stefano and, after a few metres, on your left you will see the

TORRE ALBERICI

UTILITY

Via S. Stefano

line n. 11, 13, 14, 19, 25, 28, 29, 30 (Rizzoli)

It was erected by the homonymous family in the 12th century, and still today you can see the charming shop with the fold-shaped wooden serraglia (arch keystone), that was preserved during the restoration of 1928 in place of the original base.

On the façade visitors can clearly observe the scaffolding holes that are typical of Bologna in Middle Ages.

The scaffolding holes of the Bologna's towers had practical usefulness in tower's life, since they were employed in many ways:

to secure the scaffolds during the construction; to embed the wooden beams used as platforms and stairs so as to connect the tower's levels, and also to make the same tower communicate with the nearby towers owned by friendly families.

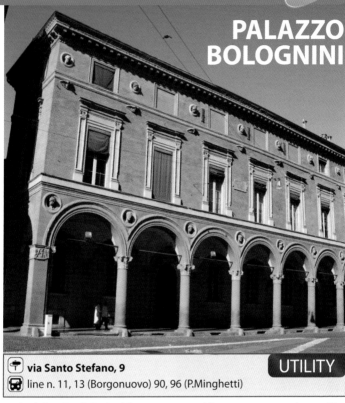

continue walking along Via S.Stefano, and when this road reaches the square, the palace you will see on your right is the

PALAZZO BOLOGNINI

via Santo Stefano, 9

line n. 11, 13 (Borgonuovo) 90, 96 (P.Minghetti)

UTILITY

The left side of the building was erected between 1517 and 1551. The design was attributed to Formigine, while the le sculptures in the capitals are attributed to the same Formigine and to Properzia de' Rossi. The right side of the building was erected around 1602. The marvellous 15th century façade was realized by the Tuscan artist Pagno di Lapo Portigiani. During the 16th century Alfonso Lombardi and Nicolò da Volterra made it peculiar by fitting a series of terracotta fanciful heads, while in the following period Giulio Cesare Colventi worked there. The building was completed in 1884, after it had been acquired in 1842 by the Isolani family, proprietor of an adjoining palace. The unification of the two palaces makes the building spread from Strada Maggiore to Piazza Santo Stefano.

The Bolognini family, whose exponents were rich silk merchants, was one of the Bologna's most important families of the 15th century, that so greatly contributed to the artistic growth of the city. One of the chapels present in the Basilica di San Petronio, the Cappella Bolognini, was built by Bartolomeo Bolognini at the beginning of the 15th century.

The recent threats of Islamic extremists due to the representation of Mohammed in the Hell within the chapel's frescoes, have caused the same chapel to hit the headlines. Actually, Mohammed is represented as an old man with white beard, who is completely naked, tied up and tortured by a demon, and also surrounded by other sinners.

Right in front there is the

BI-15
MP3

BASILICA DI SANTO STEFANO

UTILITY

Via S. Stefano, 24 **Museo di Santo Stefano:**
+39.051.223256 Working days: 9-12.30 and 15.30-18.30;
Holidays: 9-13 and 15.30-19 free limited line n. 11, 13, 20, 29, 30, 90, 96 (P.Minghetti) C (Borgonuovo)

It is located at 24 Via Santo Stefano.

In Bologna it is known as Basilica delle sette chiese (Basilica of the seven churches), which is a monumental complex of buildings called "Sacred Jerusalem". Legend attributes the foundation of the Church to the Bologna's Bishop Petronio, who ruled the Diocese from 431 to 450. He is deemed to have commissioned a reproduction of the places of the Passion of Christ to dedicate them to the Christian proto-martyr Stephen, that had visited them during his travel to the Holy Land. It features the Romanesque, early Christian, Byzantine, Longobard, Frankish and Othonian styles. The basilica stands in the spot where the remains of the Saints Vitalis and Agricola are kept. In the church you can admire, among other artworks, the "Stoning of Saint Stephen" by Cittadini, a "Pietà" by the sculptor Po', and the "Madonna of Snow" attributed to Lippo di Dalmasio. The complex of Santo Stefano also contains a museum, with paintings, frescos and relics.

At the centre of the Church, in the aedicule below, there are the remains of Saint Petronius, except for the head that is kept in the metropolitan church dedicated to him.

Continue walking along Via S.Stefano and pass the large crossroads, after a few tens of metres the palace on your right is the

FORMER TEATRO DEL CORSO

UTILITY

📍 via Santo Stefano, 33

🚌 line n. 11, 13, C
(Garganelli)

It was erected in 1805 on a design by Francesco Santini, and was inaugurated in June of that year, in the presence of Napoleon. The interior was completely destroyed by a bombing in 1944.

A CURIOUS NOTE

On 21st June 1805 Napoleon Bonaparte triumphally ntered the city at three o'clock of the afternoon, after the traditional artillery shot, while all the city's bells were ringing.

After refusing the city's keys, that the president of the municipality offered him, since "… they were lying in the right hands…", he reached the Palazzo Caprara, going by through two wings of soldiers and accompanied by the applause of the crowd and the hymns in his honour.

On the night of that day the city was fully illuminated for the occasion, and the celebrations continued inside the Teatro del Corso, where Napoleon Bonaparte and Giuseppina Beauharnais attended the *Serious Opera* and the ball in their honour, afterwards they withdrew to their lodgings.

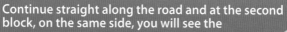

PALAZZO VIZZANI

📍 **via Santo Stefano, 43**

🚌 line n. 11, 13, 90, 96 (Garganelli)

UTILITY

The building dates back to the second half of the 16th century, and was rebuilt on a design by Bartolomeo Triachini. In the background of the courtyard there are traces of *perspective decorations* by A. Galli Bibiena.

The hall houses *oval paintings* by L. Sabbatini, while the loggia holds the *"Blinding of Polyphemus"*, a work by L. Samacchini dating back to 1570.

In 1732 it became property of Cardinal Lambertini, and on the noble floor it was decorated with 18th century *frescoes* by F. Minozzi, C. Lodi, P. Dardani and stuccos by P. Tadolini; in other halls there are *paintings* by A. Basoli and F. Giani going back to the 1822. Today it houses the Presidency of the Faculty of Foreign Language and Literature of the University of Bologna.

A CURIOUS NOTE

The immense artistic possessions and the magnificent wealth of the Vizzani family are well described in the will that a great-grandchild of Pompeo drew up before the notary Bernardino Ugolotti, in 1640.

The library, the contents of which have been lost, included not only hundreds of books, but also clocks, world maps, mathematical instruments, etc. (it must not be forgot that, from 1563, it had been the venue for the literary and scientific disputes of the Accademia degli Oziosi, founded by the Vizzani family).

Continue straight along the road and at the following block, on the same side, you will see the

PALAZZO BOSDARI AGUCCHI

via Santo Stefano, 75

line n. 11, 13, 90, 96 (Garganelli)

UTILITY

Only the beautiful façade with balcony was realized according to the design by Carlo Francesco Dotti (1740). Its brick wall face is covered with a thin layer of cocciopesto shaving, while the architectural elements consist of sandstone appropriately shaped and characterized by a series of surface coverings.

The palace does not feature the honour staircase initially designed by Dotti, and at the back it was completed by Angelo Venturoli in 1795.

A CURIOUS NOTE

In 1831 one exponent of this Bologna's senatorial family, Count Alessandro Agucchi, took part in the "*Provisional Commission of Government*", compiled by the lawyer Antonio Zanolini for want of the Papal Prolegate. The commission consisted of eight members, partly Carbonaros and partly moderate liberals, who all were notable citizens. The crucial event that forced the Prolegate to this decision was the rising occurred in Piazza Maggiore on the morning of February 4th. There a crowd of Liberals gathered together to acclaim Italy and freedom, and at the same time asked the establishment of a civic guard.

The following day, February 5th 1831, the Church's coats of arms were lowered from the public palace and also in Bologna the Italian tricolour was hoisted.

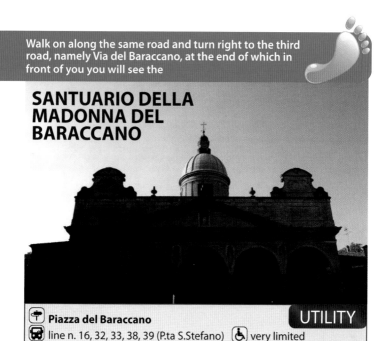

Walk on along the same road and turn right to the third road, namely Via del Baraccano, at the end of which in front of you you will see the

SANTUARIO DELLA MADONNA DEL BARACCANO

Piazza del Baraccano

UTILITY

line n. 16, 32, 33, 38, 39 (P.ta S.Stefano) very limited

The current building was commissioned by Annibale Bentivoglio and built in 1512, thus enlarging and embellishing a little chapel that housed the image of the Madonna painted by Lippo di Dalmasio on the city's defensive walls.

The dome dates back to 1682 and was executed by Ambrosi.

The elegant façade with the 16th century portico still holds the figures of the Bologna's patron saints dating back to the first construction. In the tympanum there is an image of the Madonna of the Lombards.

In the interior the nave is parallel to the façade since the sanctuary has been built close to the city's walls.

The image of the "Madonna and Child" attributed to Lippo di Dalmasio was formerly located in the great tower called Baraccano, and now it is on the main altar, framed with pieces of marble sculpted by Properzia de' Rossi and Sigismondo Bergellesi.

It was almost entirely painted again in 1472 by the Ferrara's artist Francesco Cossa.

Still today, the Sanctuary is the destination for pilgrims and for the newly married couples who go there to "take the peace", namely to implore for marital peace by kissing a miniature image representing the Madonna by Cossa, and by offering flowers on the altar dedicated to the Virgin Mary. Tradition suggests that the bride has to leave her own bouquet on the altar.

Nearby you see the former Conservatorio delle Putte del Baraccano (*Maids' Conservatory of Baraccano*) overlooking Via Santo Stefano. Nowadays the ancient Chiesa delle Putte is the seat of the Civic Centre of the Santo Stefano district.

In 1553, the Conservatorio delle Putte del Baraccano was essentially engaged in giving hospitality to female children and unmarried girls,

most of whom had remained orphans as a consequence of the terrible plague epidemic of 1527. The deep devotion to the Virgin Mary found expression in safeguarding and preserving the purity of the young girls hosted there.

The Conservatory gave hospitality, educated and created profits from the artisan bent of the orphan girls, with the only objective to grant them a dowry and a future social integration.

The veils and laces manufactured by the Baraccano's maids were goods especially appreciated by the market of that time, as long as the silk production and commerce were one of the leading sectors of Bologna's economy.

After exiting the church take the road on your left, Via Orfeo, continue straight until the fourth crossing, there turn right and pass under the *Torresotto* in Via Castiglione. Then, after a few tens of metres, on your right you will see the

FORMER CHIESA DI SANTA LUCIA

via Castiglione, 36
line n. C (Cestello)

UTILITY

It was erected by the Jesuits from 1623 according to a design by Girolamo Rainaldi. The single-nave majestic interior refers to the layout of the Chiesa del Gesù in Rome, with a rich stucco decoration. The façade, the apse section and the dome remained unfinished. The current apse was realized by Vincenzo Vannini (1840). Inside visitors can admire a "Madonna and Child" realized by the sculptor Giuseppe Mazza. The church was renovated in 1988, now it is used as Lecture Theatre of the University.

A CURIOUS NOTE

In 1562, through a papal bull, Pope Pius IV donated the little parish Chiesa di S. Lucia to the Jesuits.

The objective of this project was to offer to the Jesuits, who had previously settled down in some nearby houses, a place that could become the centre of their spiritual education activity. Actually, this was the Order preferred by the Pope.

After a few years, the Collegio di Santa Lucia was erected in the vicinity. This also was assigned to the Order. Towards the end of the 18th century, thanks to donations, bequests and acquisitions, all the buildings located between the church and Via Cartoleria had slowly become property of the Jesuits, who were so able to complete their initial project with the construction of the convent, the library, the schools and the portico to Via Castiglione.

The suppression of the Order realized by Pope Clement XIV with the bull *"Dominus ac Redemptor"*, issued on August 16th 1773, caused the whole complex to be handed over to the Barnabite Fathers.

The Napoleon's suppression left the Barnabites only the church that, after the establishment of the Kingdom of Italy, was deconsecrated and became property of the Municipality.

Take Via Castiglione again and walk towards the city's centre, turn right to second side street, Via Monticelli and, after a short zigzag route, in front of you you will see the

CHIESA DI SAN GIOVANNI IN MONTE OLIVETO

📍 **Piazza San Giovanni in Monte, 1/2**   UTILITY

Museo di San Giovanni in Monte: ☎ +39.051.263894

ℹ️ Visits only on request   ♿ very limited   🚌 line n. 11, 13

(P.Minghetti) 90, 96 (Garganelli) C (Borgonuovo)

This Church is located on the homonymous square, which is some metres above the surrounding roads.

The construction is deemed to have been started in 1433, and its origin is linked to the presence of the Bishop Petronio in Bologna and to the symbols of the sacred places of Jerusalem, which he promoted (one of the seven churches). Actually, it seems that this church was built to be reminiscent of the Basilica of Ascension erected by Constantine and Saint Helena on the

Mount of Olives.

It stands on a little hill outside the first circle of city's walls and it had to be the destination of a small pilgrimage or walks.

It was enlarged in 1286 according to the Cistercian style, afterwards the side chapels and then the Renaissance chapels were built.

This was certainly a small church with concentric layout, at the centre of which stood a cross indicating the place of the Ascension of Christ.

<u>Today it is</u> divided into three naves by means of eight octagonal pillars.

<u>The chapels</u> house artworks by Guercino and painters belonging to the Bolognese school, and visitors can also admire a copy of the Saint Cecilia by Raffaello executed by Clemente Alberti. <u>The facade</u>, started in 1441, had a portico supported by lions. It was finished in 1474 and decorated with the beautiful terracotta eagle moulded by Nicolò dell'Arca (1494).

In 1797 Napoleon appropriated the building and used it as a **Prison** and seat of a **Special tribunal**. Afterwards only the political prison remained, and an office of the cantonal police was placed there. All buildings underwent a renovation on the occasion of the ninth centenary of the University of Bologna

Walk down the slope ending in Via Farini and turn left, at the first crossing turn right and, after a few tens of metres, on your right you will see the

BI-13-2
MP3

PALAZZO PEPOLI VECCHIO

via Castiglione, 4, 6, 8, 10 +39.051.229858
Saturday 13-19; Sunday 9-19   free   good
line n. 11, 13, 29, 30, 90, 96, (piazza Minghetti) 14, 19, 25, 27 (Rizzoli)

UTILITY

The Palazzo Pepoli Vecchio stands a few steps away from the Due Torri, in the first stretch of Via Castiglione (numbers 4, 6, 8, 10). It is a group of buildings that had belonged to one of the Bologna's most important families. The Palace, as we see it today, is the result of several architectural additions and stratifications.

The façade at number 4 is an example of Gothic architecture from the end of the 14th century. The building located at number 6 was built for want of Taddeo Pepoli starting from 1344 (the Pepoli's heraldic chess board is on the door). At number 8, on the ground floor is a 13th century loggia that was restored in 1923.

At number 10 are a grand staircase with 18th century decorations and sculptures by Antonio Schiassi, and halls housing tempera paintings from that same epoch.

This family, the founder of which is considered to be Romeo Pepoli, ruled the city until 1350.

Romeo was born around 1250 in a family of money-changers. His father Zerra lent money to the students of the Studium, i.e. the University. However, the number of students had been progressively decreasing from the second half of the 13th century. The nose of Romeo shifted the business target towards the consumer loans, by financing the communities of the countryside and the real estate investments. Thus the family acquired lands in the areas of San Giovanni in Persiceto, Sant'Agata Bolognese, Castel San Pietro, and in 1276 also acquired a house in Via Castiglione, that would become the first nucleus of the family's residence. The loans granted to the communities of the countryside were used by the inhabitants to pay the levies imposed by the Municipality of Bologna. These sums were almost never repaid, thus allowing the Pepoli family to become proprietor of lands and real estate.

He also lent money to the Guastavillani and Zovenzoni families, who were money-changers needing liquidity. The unscrupulousness of Romeo led him to be accused of usury and tax evasion, since he had declared an income much lower than the real one, for all this he made enemies.

PALAZZO PEPOLI CAMPOGRANDE

UTILITY

- via Castiglione, 7;
- tel. +39.051.229858;
- **Quadreria Zambeccari:** (hours subject to changes, calling is recommended) Saturday 13-19; Sunday 9-19
- free
- good
- line n. 11, 13, 29, 30, 90, 96, (piazza Minghetti) 14, 19, 25, 27 (Rizzoli)

It was built by Count Odoardo Pepoli from the second half of the 17th century onwards, and the large building was completed towards the end of that century.

The façade facing Via Castiglione was realized by the architect Francesco Albertoni.

The monumental façade facing Via Clavature was realized by the architect Giuseppe Antonio Torri, who also completed the building.

From 1670 onwards it was magnificently frescoed by Domenico Maria Canuti, an Italian painter of the Baroque period, and by Donato Creti, one of the most refined 18th century painters of Bologna.

On the grand staircase, illustrations of the medieval magnificence of the Pepoli family are displayed: *"Taddeo Pepoli is appointed Lord of Bologna"* and *"Taddeo Pepoli is confirmed as city's Vicar"*, admirably realized by Domenico Maria Canuti and dating back to 1665.

The fourth hall houses a work by Donato Creti: *"Alexander cutting the Gordian knot"* from 1710.

In the Honour Hall visitors can admire the *"Apotheosis of Hercules"* and, inside the adjoining little chapel, the "*Miracle of the She-Mule*" (taken from the hagiography of Saint Antony), located on the altar. Both artworks were realized by Canuti in 1670.

The following hall houses the admirable "*Allegory of Felsina*", a work by the brothers Rolli dating back to around 1690.

Going more ahead, visitors will find the ceilings of the two halls with the "*Triumph of Hercules with the four seasons*" and the "*Olympus*", by the master Giuseppe Maria Crespi.

Then you walk through the hall housing a *fresco* by Donato Creti, which leads back to the grand staircase.

The imposing halls of the noble floor also house the Quadreria Zambeccari, that the marquis Giacomo donated to the State at the end of the 19th century.

It contains important works by authors who were leaders of the Emilian painting, such as Ludovico Carracci, Guercino, Alessandro Tiarini, Francesco Albani, Giuseppe Maria Crespi, Bartolomeo Passerotti, Mastelletta, Marcantonio Franceschini, Lorenzo Pasinelli and Donato Creti.

A CURIOUS NOTE

In March of 1680 the Bologna's senator Odoardo Pepoli died. Since his firstborn had already died, the natural candidate to succeed him as senator was his grandson Ercole.

Following the routine procedure, the Secretariat of State asked the legate for his opinion and information about the candidate, especially as regards to any pending suit. The pro tempore legate, Girolamo Gastaldi, answered that Ercole had been actually sentenced to death and the confiscation of his property due to the murder of the notary Giuseppe Carlo Beltrami, occurred on October 9th 1678.

However, Gastaldi added that, neither before nor after this event, Ercole overdid, thus always behaving properly and acting chivalrously, without any kind of deviations. So he felt like recommending that unconditional pardon was granted to him - this was necessary in order that the senatorial title could be conferred on him.

In January of 1682 Ercole took the senate seat that had been occupied by his grandfather.

In the opinion of the canon Ghiselli, the criminal record of Ercole was actually much longer than the legate Gastaldi thought - or appeared to think.

Take Via Castiglione again and walk towards the two towers until, at number 1, you will see the

PALAZZO BOLOGNETTI

UTILITY

 via Castiglione, 1

line n. 14, 19, 25, 27 (Rizzoli)

Its construction dates back to the 16th century. It features a Bologna's Renaissance architecture, which is especially remarkable thanks to the abundance and refinement of the sandstone decorations animating its front, sides and, mainly, its interior.

To recall the reconstruction carried out by Camillo Bolognetti in 1551, a memorial slab supported by two small putti is placed on a window on the palace's left side, in the highest point.

During the reconstruction the portico of the pre-existing building, dating back to the previous century, was preserved. The authorship of the building's architecture is a much debated question: some assigned it to Andrea Marchesi da Formigine, while others assigned it to Pellegrino Ribaldi, and others to Antonio Moranti ("*il Terribilia*").

The palace was then handed over to the Rambaldi family, and suffered serious damages due to two bombs in the Second World War (as a token of this event, a chip can still be seen). The heirs of Rambaldi sold it to a certain Nino Torchi, member of the club "Bononia", who bought it together with some friends and commissioned an important renovation work carried out by two members of the club, the architect Santini and the engineer Guidotti.

Afterwards, other interventions on the external sandstone elements were necessary, that further embellished the structure and, more recently, the interior underwent a renovation work.

It is still the seat of the club Bonomia.

Also the Bolognetti family is included among the "Bologna's senatorial families".

Between 1466 and 1797, these noble families represented the city's most important administrative body that ruled the city together with the "pontifical Legate".

The senator title was for life, and from the 17th century onwards it also became hereditary for the firstborn, even though only in a few privileged families, it being understood that the Pope's ratification of the new senators was required.

Continue straight towards the city's centre and, after a few metres, you will reach the starting point that is also the end of this tour.

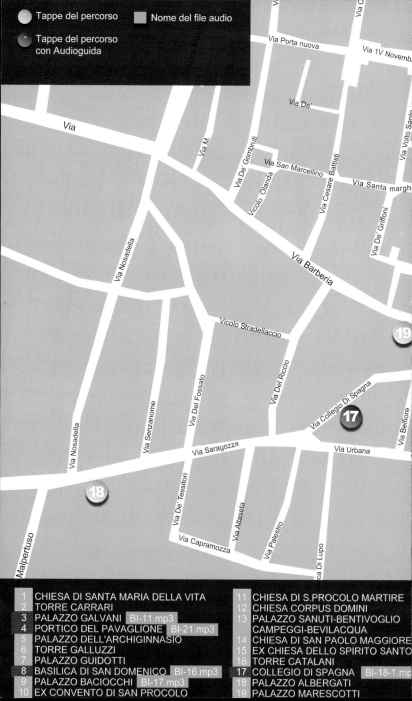

Tappe del percorso

Tappe del percorso con Audioguida

Nome del file audio

Also this tour starts from Piazza Maggiore. Keep the basilica on your right and take the narrow road in front of you, Via Clavature, walk on until you reach the crossing where, on your left, you will see the

CHIESA DI SANTA MARIA DELLA VITA

Via Clavature, 10 ☎ +39.051.236.245   **UTILITY**
Mon-Sat 7.30-19 and 16-19 Sunday and Holidays 16.30-19;
very limited
line n. 11, 20, 25, 27, 29, 30 (Rizzoli) A (P.Maggiore)

The church was founded in the second half of the 13th century by the Confraternity of the Beaten of the S. Maria della Vita, one of the first confraternities sprung up in Italy following the movement of the Disciplinati, arisen in 1260 in Perugia thanks to the thrust of Raniero Fusani. Its members nursed pilgrims and sick people in the adjoining hospital, today no longer standing.

The church was enlarged between 1454 and 1502, and rebuilt by the architect Giovan Battista Bergonzoni at the end of the 17th century, after a devastating fall of the ceiling occurred in 1686. the dome was erected in 1787 according to a design by Giuseppe Tubertini.

The interior has an elliptical layout, and there visitors can admire the famous "*statuesque group of the Pietà*", one of the most energetic and expressive masterpieces of Italian sculpture, moulded by Nicolò dell'Arca in the second half of the 15th century, and sculptures by Acquisti.

On the main altar there is the fresco representing the Madonna of Life, dating back to the second half of the 14th century.

A CURIOUS NOTE

"Beaten" is the name of the members of several medieval lay confraternities, and it derives from the penance of flagellation they inflicted on themselves as a rule. The "Beaten" devoted themselves to works of charity and assistance, especially by managing hospices and hospitals and attending religious rites. These groups were particularly widespread in the towns of Northern Italy, especially in Veneto. The hierarchical organization usually included the "*castaldo*" as the head, who was supported by a treasurer (*massaro*) and the director of the hospital (*priore - prior*). Also women actively participated therein, and it is even said that there were some female *priors*. They normally were the wives of deceased priors who took up their tasks. These confraternities were very active as long as they existed, however in several cases they were suppressed by the Napoleon's edicts at the beginning of the 19th century.

Continue straight on until you reach the next crossing, then take Via Marchesana on the right, walk half of the road approximately where, on your left, you will see the

TORRE CARRARI

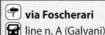

| via Foscherari | UTILITY |
| line n. A (Galvani) | |

It is a *casatorre* erected by the Carrari family at the turn of the 13th century. The *casetorri* combined a greater habitability, solidity, hygiene and safety of inhabitants.

At those times the Carrari family owned a large part of the area located between the current roads de' Toschi, Marchesana and Foscherari, including the church, the tower and the *casatorre*. Afterwards, the church and the *casatorre* were handed over to the Foscherari family (maybe there existed an hereditary line: Fosco Carrari ?), after whom the neighbouring road was named.

Continue straight along Via Marchesana until you reach the crossing with Via Foscherari, turn right and, at the end of the road, turn right to the portico and, after a few metres, you will find the

BI-11
MP3

PALAZZO GALVANI

Museo Civico Archeologico

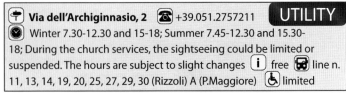

📍 **Via dell'Archiginnasio, 2** ☎ +39.051.2757211 **UTILITY**

🕐 Winter 7.30-12.30 and 15-18; Summer 7.45-12.30 and 15.30-18; During the church services, the sightseeing could be limited or suspended. The hours are subject to slight changes ℹ free 🚌 line n. 11, 13, 14, 19, 20, 25, 27, 29, 30 (Rizzoli) A (P.Maggiore) ♿ limited

It houses artworks by Aldrovandi, Cospi, Marsili, the Bologna's painter Pelagio Pelagi, as well as works coming from the University of Bologna and Etruscan tombs, which were found both on urban excavations and in the surrounding territory. Currently it includes about 200,000 artworks divided into sections, one of which is dedicated to Egypt.

A CURIOUS NOTE

The **Museo Civico Archeologico** was opened to the public in 1881 and it is housed inside the Palazzo Galvani (former "Ospedale di Santa Maria della Morte"). The Ospedale della Morte was divided into different sections: men, women and injured people. It also had rooms used as schools for physicians, and even an ice-house. The students of Medicine, who in the nearby Palazzo dell'Archiginnasio studied anatomy by using the cadavers of the executed people, also frequented the hospital regularly.

The confraternity that gave origin to the name Santa Maria della Morte arose in 1336. They dedicated themselves to assist the prisoners and those condemned to death, while their coat of arms had three skulls surmounted by a cross with hanging scourges.

Ever since the 15th century the Confraternita di Santa Maria della Morte (Confraternity of Saint Mary of Death) was closely linked to the cult of the Madonna di San Luca, and as long as it existed, it was engaged in organizing both the procession that brought the Madonna from the Colle della Guardia to the city, and the processions through the city's districts, as well as in keeping the icon during the nights it remained in the city. In 1798 the Napoleon's laws dissolved this Confraternity.

After exiting the museum, turn left and you will be already in the

BI-21
MP3

PORTICO DEL PAVAGLIONE

It derived its name from Bologna's dialectal word "*pavaian*", used to indicate the important popular market of the cocoons, which was housed in the palace in front of the portico and attracted people from everywhere. The portico measures 139 metres in length and was built by Antonio Morandi in 1562 at request of Pope Pius IV. It has always been the favourite place for the worldly walks of the Bologna's citizens.

A CURIOUS NOTE

The porticos are the evident characteristic of Bologna (more than 38 kilometres inside the city's walls). In the face of the population growth, in the late Middle Ages the portico became the more immediate, economically  accessible and urbanistically convenient solution, to allow the city's dwellings to enlarge. The building costs had to be totally paid by the private citizens, and the construction could not be realized on public land. Originally the supporting pillars were made out of wood, later they were replaced by stone columns in order to better their structural safety.

Over the years, the porticos took also the role of refuge and meeting place for the passers-by, as well as temporary extension of artisan shops.

Walk on along the portico and on your left you will find the

PALAZZO dell'ARCHIGINNASIO

 Piazza Galvani, 1   📞 +39.051.276811   `UTILITY`
🕐 **Palazzo e Teatro Anatomico**: Mon-Fri 9-18.45 Saturday: 9-13.45,
🕐 **Sala dello Stabat Mater**: Mon-Sat 9-13.30 ask the doorkeeper,
closed: Sunday, Christmas, New Year's Day and Easter; line n. 11,
13, 14, 19, 25, 27, 29, 30 (Rizzoli), A (P.Galvani), 16, 30, 38, 39, 52, 58, 59,
navette A (P.Cavuor); very limited

It was erected in 1562 at the request of Pope Pius IV, who put pressure on the Papal Deputy Legate Pier Donato Cesi, in order to have a single university's seat where the type of lessons given could be easily controlled, so that they were not in contrast with the clerical dogma of that epoch. The palace was designed by the Bologna's famous architect Antonio Morandi and was finished within only two years, then from 1563 to 1803 it housed the seat of the University of Bologna.

It is an elegant building with a facade 149 metres long, and with 30 arches in the portico (the Pavaglione) which represents the symbol of the Bologna's culture. In the courtyard of the palace visitors can admire *thousands of coats of arms* representing families, chancellors and other personages who attended the "Studio". Actually, ever since the last century the most eminent masters of the university studied and taught here. On the single floor of the palace there

still are the two Lecture Theatres (*Aula Magna degli Artisti*, today the reading hall of the civic library, and *Aula dei Legisti*, called *Stabat Mater* following the performance of the famous opera by Rossini carried out in 1842) with the image of the Madonna on the desks.

Another important hall is the *Teatro anatomico*, where the anatomy lessons were held. The desk is also significant thanks to its canopy supported by two men without skin (*the Spellati*). Before the French Revolution public medicine lessons were held in this palace during carnival time. Until the end of the 18th century, in the palace's courtyard the "Teriaca" was produced. It was a medicine that, at those times, was considered to be prodigious thanks to the wide range of diseases it said to heal. Inside an enormous pot the "Speziale" (i.e. the chemist) boiled an

infusion consisting of an indefinite and secret number of ingredients, and at the end of this process the medicine was obtained.

In 1838 it became the Civic Library, and now it is one of the most well-furnished libraries in Europe

The Studium, that represents the most ancient European University, sprang as free organization of students who personally chose and paid the professors. In order to help one another, the students formed colleges consisting of mates from the same country (nationes), divided into *intramontani* (or *citramontani*) and *ultramontani*. Ever since the 12th century there were already 17 *intramontane* and 14 *ultramontane subnationes*. As a future evidence of that, the Palazzo dell'Archiginnasio (that was the seat of the first University) keeps a heraldic complex made up of around 6,000 students' coats of arm. In contrast to the Bologna's model, that was original in that epoch, was the model from Paris, where the Universities of masters were linked to the Church and the monarchic authority. The evolution of the lay university caused the professors' salary to be paid by the Municipality of Bologna.

In the 16th century the university spirit, always quick to make fun of anybody, invented the stock character of Dottor "*Balanzone*", an ignorant man assuming an attitude of great learned figure

After exiting the Archiginnasio, cross the square and enter the vault in front of you, then you will see the

TORRE GALLUZZI

🏛 **Corte Galluzzi**	**UTILITY**
🚌 line n. 11, 13, 20, 30, 38, 39 (Farini) A (Galvani)	

The Torre Galluzzi, a Casatorre dating back to the 12th century, together with its companions Prendiparte and Azzoguidi towers, is part of the so-called (pro-papal) Guelph triad. Currently it is 30 metres high (originally it is was higher), and its toughness gave a sense of solidity indicating power and wealth. It is located inside a single building group, that at that epoch was called "curia", namely a complex consisting of the dwellings, the gentilitial chapel, and the towers of a same family.

Inside visitors can see the type of masonry, pointed out by an excellent renovation work, while outside they can see the original door of the building that opens more than six metres off the ground.

Walk back to Piazza Galvani, cross it and turn immediately right. When you reach the crossing, turn left to Via Farini, walk on until the square on your right, then the building you will see on the corner in front of you is the

PALAZZO GUIDOTTI

Piazza Cavour, 1 (also accessible from Via Farini, 9) **UTILITY**
line n. 11, 13, 38, 39 (Farini) 16, 30, 52, 59, A (piazza Cavour)

The building side facing Via Cavour was designed by Coriolano Monti and Antonio Zannoni in 1866 following the 19th century rearrangement of the whole area, aimed at realizing the new Piazza Cavour, obtained through the demolition of the ancient roads Borgo Salamo, dei Libri, Miola and of the Chiesa di Sant'Andrea degli Ansaldi.

This was a Bologna's ancient senatorial family, which had Alessandro Guidotti, an Italian patriot and general (Bologna, 1790 – Treviso, 1848), among its most recent descendants.

After taking part in several campaigns as a member of the retinue of Napoleon I, King of Italy, he was taken prisoner during the retreat from the Russia's campaign. He did not suffer many afflictions thanks to the benevolence he gained through his culture from some local families. Once he came back to Italy in 1814, he immediately put himself into service with Gioacchino Murat.

After the fall of the Empire of Napoleon, he retired to private life. However, due to his liberal ideas, the policemen of the Papal government and the Austrian troops always kept an eye on him.

Keep the Palazzo Guidotti on your left, walk back along the portico and, at the end, cross the road and take the narrow road in front of you. It leads to the Piazza S.Domenico, where you will see the

BI-16
MP3

BASILICA di SAN DOMENICO

📍 **Piazza S. Domenico, 13**

UTILITY

Museo di Santo Domenico: ☎ +39.051.6400411 🕐 Mon-Fri 9.30-12.30 and 15.30-18.30; Saturday and Holidays 15.30-17.30 ℹ free ♿ limited 🚌 line n. 16, 30, 38, 39, 52, 58, 59, A (P.Cavuor)

It belongs to the Order of Dominican friars.

The Convent and the Church were built in Romanesque style during the 13th century.

It houses artworks by important artists, among whom there are Giunta and Nicolò Pisano, Nicolò dell'Arca, Michelangelo, Jacopo da Bologna, Guido Reni, Guercino and Filippo Lippi.

The church features <u>three naves</u>, some <u>side chapels</u>, a <u>transept</u> and a <u>chorus</u>. *The main altar* was executed by Torreggiani in the 18th century, and behind the altar visitors can admire a monumental wooden chorus.

The church houses precious artworks, such as a "*Crucifix*" by Giunta Pisano, the "*Mystic Marriage of Saint Catherine*" by Filippo Lippi, the "*Saint Raymond*" of Penafort crossing the sea over his cloak by Lodovico Carracci, and the "*Saint Thomas Aquinas*" by Guercino.

The basilica moreover houses the organ used by Wolfang Amadeus Mozart during his stay in Bologna, and other precious organs, even if not all are functioning.

The Basilica has a *small museum* of artworks and relics, and it also holds valuable manuscripts.

It was founded by Saint Dominic of Guzman who had come to Bologna in order to promote the Dominican order after the acknowledgment by Pope Honorius III.

Initially Saint Dominic and his monks settled in a church located outside the walls, then due to lack of space they moved to the Convento di San Nicolò della Vergine, where today sits the basilica and where Saint Dominic died.

A CURIOUS NOTE

In the Middle Ages the city of Bologna housed one of the four main universities in Europe: the University of Oxford excelled in science, the University of Paris excelled in theology and philosophy, the University of Montpellier excelled in medicine, while the University of Bologna was considered par excellence the seat of law. Ever since its origin the Dominican Order (or Order of Preachers), the Constitutions of which refer to the cultural ferments and the democratic spirit typical of the first medieval Italian Municipalities, had participated in the arising and growing of the most important universities: this is the reason why in 1218 Saint Dominic decided to found in Bologna a convent that would have become a religious, intellectual and cultural reference point.

After exiting the Basilica, take Via Garibaldi on the left. This road leads to Piazza Tribunali, where the palace in front of you is the

BI-17
MP3

PALAZZO BACIOCCHI

⚐ **Piazza Tribunali, 4**

🚌 line n. 16, 30, 38, 39, 59, A (Tribunale)

UTILITY

It is the current Palace of Justice.

The initial design belonged to Andrea Palladio and was executed in 1534.

The construction was continued by other local artists even after the death of Palladio, and it was notably supplemented between the 17th and the 19th centuries.

Actually, in 1679 the palace was acquired by the Ranuzzi family, that enlarged and embellished it with artworks.

The most important ones are:

The great staircase of honour with the two elliptical flights is attributed to Giovanni Battista Piacentini. The allegorical stucco statues were added around 1770.

The Feasting hall (now Hall of the Court of Appeal) was designed by Ferdinando Bibiena at the beginning of the 18th century; the allegorical statues were executed by Giuseppe Maria Mazza, while the stucco decorations were the work of G. Borrelli.

The Gallery, also designed by G. B. Piacentini, was officially inaugurated in 1727.

The last owner was Felice Baciocchi who, being a merchant, was invested by Napoleon with the title of Prince when he married Napoleon's sister Elisa.

He completed the palace by commissioning important painters, such as Antonio Basoli, Felice Giani and others, to revive the memories of the regime of his brother-in-law.

It is one of the most beautiful palaces in Bologna.

A CURIOUS NOTE

Both the Ruini and the Ranuzzi family, that owned the palace before the Baciocchi family, belonged to the Bologna's senatorial families, namely noble families that, between 1466 and 1797, were part of the Bologna's Senate, the highest government organ of Bologna together with the papal Legate. The senator title was always for life, although starting from the <u>17th century</u> it became de facto hereditary within a few noble families, unless they fell into disfavour with the papal court, that had always to confirm the appointment of the new senators.

Keep the Palazzo Baciocchi on your left, walk on and take Via Tovaglie. Walk through this road until the end in Via d'Azeglio, then turn right, there the building on the corner on your right is the

FORMER CONVENTO DI SAN PROCOLO

🕈 via d'Azeglio, 56   🚌 line n. 29, 52 (S.Procolo)   UTILITY

This Benedictine monastery, that dated back to the 11th century, was erected around the 16th and 17th centuries.

The complex consists of *three cloisters* built according to a design by Giacomo and Benedetto dalla Torre in 1547, by Domenico Tibaldi in 1577 and by Giulio dalla Torre from 1613 to 1628.

The refectory houses the "*Miraculous fishing*" frescoed by Lionello Spada in 1607; other halls house *paintings* by Alessandro Tiarini (1639-40).

The conventual complex, that drew its origin from an ancient place of cult dedicated to Saint Proculus, became soon one of the richest and most important monasteries in Bologna, also thanks to its relationship with the schools of law. The Convento di San Procolo was the most ancient seat of the Universitas of the jurist pupils.

The convent was renovated and enlarged from around 1550, and during the 16th and 17th centuries it reached the current layout. The monastery not only was the reference centre for Bologna's culture, but it also became a city's important economic centre.

Over the following epochs, the complex underwent many changes and adjustments related to the different ways it was used: namely, it was transformed into *barracks for the city's troops* after the Napoleon's suppression of 1796, then it was reconverted in a hospital (the *Ospedale degli Esposti*) until 1860, afterwards it became the seat of the *Asilo di Maternità* (the Refuge of Maternity), and finally the seat of the *Ospedale della Maternità* (the *Maternity Hospital*). This destination was kept until the end of the 20th century, when the Maternity Ward was moved to the Ospedale Maggiore of Bologna. Subsequently, the premises of the former Convent were freed, and soon they will be renovated in order to be transformed into a high-level tourist accommodation structure.

A CURIOUS NOTE

Between the end of the 14th century and the beginning of the 15th century, in the former convent the Ospizio degli Esposti is created, that remained so until the middle of the 19th century.

The "Esposti" were orphans, often sons of single mothers who were not able or did not want to take care of the babies, and put them in care of the "wheel", namely the convent's revolving door. This system guaranteed the anonymity, thus allowing these "little bastards" to be abandoned into the hands of the nuns.

It was also a shelter for those single mothers who had to hide their pregnancy, and knocked on the convent door in order to stay and hide themselves there during the whole pregnancy period, afterwards they abandoned their newborn children.

Continue straight along the road and, at the end of the former Convent, you will reach the

CHIESA DI SAN PROCOLO MARTIRE

🚏 via d'Azeglio, 52   **UTILITY**

🚌 line n. 20, 38, 39 (Urbana) 29, 52 (S.Procolo)

It is one of the most ancient churches of the Benedictine order in Bologna.

The current building was erected toward the middle of the 12th century and was dedicated to Saint Proculus, one of the first martyrs of Bolognese Christian tradition. It holds the sepulchre of the Saint. This convent certainly represented a meeting place for university students, as well as a spiritual centre.

Between 14th and 15th centuries the building received a Gothic structure, which today can only be noted in the façade.

The chapels house several artworks and the tomb of Saint Proculus, dating back to the late Roman epoch. Moreover there are notable 16th and 17th century cloisters and halls.

Put your back to the Chiesa di S.Procolo, take the road in front and, at the end of it, turn left. After a few metres on you right you will see the

CHIESA CORPUS DOMINI (or della Santa)

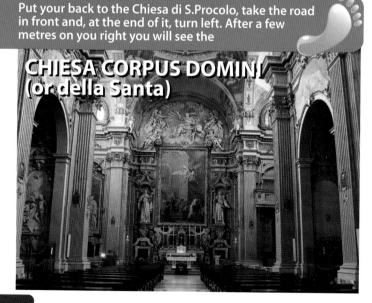

via Tagliapietre, 19 **UTILITY**
Cappella della Santa: Mar.-Gio-Sab-Dom 10-12 e 16-18
Museum: +39.051.331277 Tue-Thu-Sat-Sun 10-12 and 16-18
Sanctuary: 9.30 - 12.00 / 15.30 - 18.00 (every day) During the church
services, the sightseeing could be limited or suspended. The hours are
subject to slight changes i free limited
line n. 20, 38, 39 (Urbana) 29, 52 (S.Procolo)

It is commonly known as "*Chiesa della Santa*" due to the presence of the body of Saint Catherine de' Vigri, founder of the first convent of Poor Clare nuns in Bologna in 1456.

It is one of the city's most beloved sanctuaries in popular devotion.

It was built between 1477 and 1480 by the Tuscan artists Nicolò Marchionne da Firenze and Francesco Fucci da Doccia.

The Renaissance facade has partly remained in its natural state, and is enlivened by elegant terracotta reliefs attributed to Sperandio from Mantova.

The interior was renovated by the architect G. Giacomo Monti towards the end of the 17th century, and it had been decorated with marvellous *paintings* by M. Antonio Franceschini with *decorations* by Enrico Haffner and stucco reliefs by Giuseppe Mazza: unfortunately, the bombings of the last war ruined most part of this precious artistic complex.

Some paintings are really noteworthy, among which are the famous "*Transit of Saint Joseph*", a work from 1692 by Franceschini and Lodovico Carracci, and the *tombs* of the physicist Luigi Galvani and of Laura Bassi, a famous woman scientist living in the 18th century.

A CURIOUS NOTE

The museum holds the sitting and incorrupt body of Saint Catherine de' Vigri (1413-1463). It appears blackened by the centuries, and is displayed to believers while wearing her Franciscan habit and sitting on a golden wooden seat, which Giovanni II Bentivoglio donated to the Convent.

The body is also protected by a glass urn. This Franciscan nun founded the monastery of Corpus Domini in 1456, namely the first convent of Poor Clare nuns in Bologna.

After exiting the church, turn left and continue straight ahead until the second crossing, Via Urbana, then turn right and turn left at the first crossing. After a while you will reach the

PALAZZO SANUTI-BENTIVOGLIO-CAMPEGGI-BEVILACQUA

📍 **Via d'Azeglio, 31**

🚌 line n. 20, 38, 39, 29 (Urbana)

UTILITY

This splendid palace was built in 1477 by Nicolò Sanuti, Count of Porretta, and shows strong traces of the Tuscan influence brought to Bologna by Pagno di Lapo.

An interesting part is the *internal courtyard*, which features a portico, two loggias one over the other, and rich decorations with sculptures and terracotta relief works. When the palace passed to Bevilacqua, he made it artistically richer. It represents one of the most notable palaces in Bologna.

Moreover, it must be noted the use of rustication on the façade, like the beautiful Palazzo dei Diamanti in Ferrara.

This is the only Bologna's building in which the sandstone façade comes from the quarry at Madonna del Ponte near the Bagni della Porretta, a property of Sanuti himself.

Upon his death the building was still unfinished and, in January of 1504, his wife Nicolosia handed it over to Giovanni II Bentivoglio. In the night of November 2nd of that same year, Giovanni and his family were forced to leave Bologna (only after they came to an agreement with Louis XII of France, whose armies had been compelled to support Pope Julius II, that they would have obtained a safe shelter in Milan and maintained the possession of their fortune. Nine days later Pope Julius II triumphally entered Bologna and regained control over it).

In 1547 the palace was sold to the powerful Cardinal Lorenzo Campeggi, and three sessions of the endless Council of Trent were held there due to safety reasons (officially they intended to escape the plague that was spreading in Trentino, but the real reason was the disputes dividing Pope Paul III and Charles V).

Walk on along the road until you reach the crossing with Via Carbonesi, turn left and continue straight. Then, in the next, on the left you will see the

CHIESA DI SAN PAOLO MAGGIORE

UTILITY

📍 **via Carbonesi, 18**

☎ +39.051.331490

🕐 Working days 8-12 and 16-19; Holidays 8.30-13 and 16.30-19;

♿ very limited

🚌 line n. 20, 38, 39, (Farini) 29, 52 (Urbana)

It was erected by the Regular Clerics of Saint Paul or Barnabites between 1606 and 1611, according to a design by the brother architect Ambrogio Mazenta.

During the years 1634-36 the church was embellished with a harmonious front realized by Ercole Fichi. Towards the end of the 17th century Antonio and Giuseppe Rolli decorated the vaults by depicting the deeds of Saint Paul on the areopagus(1) of Athens.

On the altars visitors can admire valuable paintings by masters belonging to Bologna's school, among whom are Guercino, Giuseppe Maria Crespi (called "lo Spagnolo") and Lodovico Carracci, who executed the famous Paradise. On the main altar there is the admirable and vigorous sculptural group representing the Beheading of Saint Paul, a work by Alessandro Algardi from the first half of the 17th century. This same artist also realized the medallion of the altar frontal and the tabernacle.

Notes

(1) a hill located north-west of the Acropolis of Athens.

A CURIOUS NOTE

Originally, also the Barnabites, like all the new religious movements arisen in the Church, represented a problem for the established power. The cause was their religious fervour that further pointed out the lifestyle of a part of the clergy at that time.

The request of the Inquisition that the movement withdrew and assumed a profile more consistent with the models of religious life being outlined in those years by the Council of Trent, caused some to abandon, however most of Barnabites adapted themselves to the new situation.

Upon the suppression of the Order of the Jesuits, the Barnabites were asked to succeed them in the management of some organizations of the suppressed Company of Jesus (such as the Bologna's Collegio San Luigi).

However, as often it happens, the humiliation follows the glory: soon the Barnabites suffered the same fate as the Jesuits, and in 1810 a Napoleon's decree suppressed all the religious orders. This occasioned the dispersion of the Brothers, although the suppression only lasted a few years.

After exiting the church take the road in front of you and, after a few tens of metres, on your right you will see the

FORMER CHIESA (AND CONVENTO) DELLO SPIRITO SANTO

 via Val d'Aposa

 line n. 11, 13, 38, 39 (Farini)

UTILITY

It is located in Via Val d'Aposa, where the torrent Aposa flowed uncovered until 1070.

The building was erected towards 1481 at the expenses of the Celestine Fathers and the believers in order to hold a miraculous image of the Blessed Virgin, which had been found right there.

The Minor Clerics of the Holy Spirit settled down there ever since 1646, but the large convent was built in 1746, according to a design by Alfonso Torreggiani.

The adjacent church, which dated back to 1665, was redesigned by Giuseppe Jarmorini in 1788.

The beautiful 15th century terracotta reliefs of the very small façade are attributed to the sculptor Vincenzo Onori.

The interior houses remains of stucco decorations and two large statues by Filippo Scandellari.

The whole complex was seriously damaged by a bombing in 1943.

In 1957, it recovered its ancient magnificence thanks to a careful renovation work.

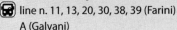

Take the alley on the church side and continue straight ahead for a few tens of metres, then you will see the

TORRE CATALANI

UTILITY

Vicolo dello Spirito Santo

line n. 11, 13, 20, 30, 38, 39 (Farini)
A (Galvani)

This is a Casatorre from the 13th century consisting of three superimposed rooms and a cellar made in the foundation perimeter.

Scholars agree that the radially

arranged bridge holes prove that each floor featured an external platform with wooden surface. Moreover, whilst the interiors were painted, also the outside were probably brightened with family gonfalons, decorations and other elements that gave vivacity to the building.

Walk back until Via Carbonesi and take the road running laterally along the right side of the Chiesa di S.Paolo Maggiore, keep on your right and walk on, then you will reach the

BI-18-1
MP3

COLLEGIO DI SPAGNA

UTILITY

via Collegio di Spagna, 4

line n. 20, 38, 39
(Collegio di Spagna)

It was the Cardinal Gil de Albornoz, great politician and scholar, who wanted to erect in Bologna, centre of culture, a college for his countrymen.

In 1370 it already began to be attended by Spanish young people and it is still today.

From the main entrance to the building, executed by Andrea da Formigine, the immunity granted to the college started.

You are recommended to visit the Oratorio di S. Clemente and the upper Loggia with glass windows, which both house several artworks.

By reading the college's statutes (the ones dating back to 1558 have been preserved) it can be inferred that it housed up to thirty Spanish students, who were not older than 21 years and Christian (without any heretical, Jewish or Muslim ancestor). Students and *sodales scholastici* (i.e., the learners) had to observe a very rigorous discipline, actually they were required to attend the meals, come back at evening, not give hospitality to women. The students could wear clothes made of black fabric, and a hood made of blackish fabric, while precious clothes and different colours were forbidden. The punishments for the failure to follow the rules ranged from a diet based on bread and water to the expulsion. The meals were abundant (bread, wine, 450 g veal meat), however it seems that they were often served cold (as the kitchen rooms were far away from the refectory)

At the corner with Via Saragozza, that you can see, turn right and continue straight, after a few hundreds of metres at number 28 you will see the

PALAZZO ALBERGATI

UTILITY

via Saragozza, 28

line n. 20, 38, 39 (Nosadella)

It was built around 1520, and consists of two connected groups. The design is attributed to Baldassarre Peruzzi,

The string course was realized by Lazzaro Casario in 1584.

On the ground floor a 17th century fresco by G. F. Gessi is housed.

Inside there are 18th century *tempera paintings* by P. Pesci, A. Rossi, S. Brizzi and frescoes by G. Valliani.

In the courtyard, at number 26, there are *decorations* dating back to the 18th century, and some Roman memorial slabs had been embedded in the wall. These recall the foundation of the Baths of Bononia by Augustus.

The Bologna's statutes mention the Albergati family for the first time in 1260.

It originally came from Zola Predosa and, over the years, several of its components occupied important administrative offices in the city as members of the *Magistracy of the Elders* and committees of *Sapientes*.

In the 15th century Nicolò Albergati, Bishop of Bologna, was beatified. In 1508, Pope Julius II granted an exponent of the family, Alberto, the title of Senator that was handed down de jure to firstborns together with the title of Marquis. A branch of the family came to an end in 1824, while the other one died out in 1885.

Turn back and walk along Via Saragozza again, take the fourth side street on the left, Via Collegio di Spagna, continue straight ahead until Via Carbonesi, then turn left and, after a few metres, on the left you will see the

PALAZZO MARESCOTTI

UTILITY

via Barberia, 4

line n. 20, 38, 39, (Farini) 29, 52 (Urbana)

Via Barberia is a Bologna's historical road along which you can find several senatorial palaces, that are full of historic memories.

One of these buildings is the Palazzo Marescotti. In 1501, during the Renaissance period, the Marescotti family attempted to gain power in Bologna by laying a plot against Giovanni II Bentivoglio, a notable figure, who later had become obtrusive. However, this attempt failed.

The Marescotti family belonged to the powerful **Arte dei Lardaroli** (A Guild having the exclusive right to sell cheese, salt meat, olive and seed oil, fresh fish, pork sausages, guts and butter), and originally their shop was near their houses located at the corner between Via Barberia and Via Collegio di Spagna.

The retaliation of Bentivoglio family, following the conspiracy they suffered, violently affected also their properties, which were destroyed.

After the escape of Giovanni II and the entrance of Pope Julius II to the city, the Municipality decided to grant a public subsidy in favour of the Marescotti family, as a partial compensation of the damages suffered, and this allowed the group of destroyed houses to be transformed into a Renaissance palace.

The arrangement of the spaces as we see them today can be attributed to the cultured Raniero, the last exponent of the family, who lived in the 17th century.

A CURIOUS NOTE

Under the portico of the Palazzo Marescotti there is a noteworthy large fresco representing the *Madonna and Child*, that the Bologna's citizens also called "Madonna of the Night" due to the habit, widespread among the wayfarers, of asking her for protection during their night movements through the city's roads.

Return to Via Carbonesi and, at the second crossing, take Via d'Azeglio on the left. At the end of this road you will reach Piazza Maggiore, which is the end of this road.

ALEXA
PORT
CLAN
HIERONY
Q
IN AVGVSTI
ANN

TOUR

5

1	PORTA MASCARELLA	13	VILLA ALDINI
2	PORTA ZAMBONI	14	PORTA SARAGOZZA
3	PORTA SAN VITALE	15	PORTICO di SAN LUCA
4	PORTA di STRADA MAGGIORE (MAZZINI)	16	VILLA SPADA
5	PORTA SANTO STEFANO	17	SANTUARIO BEATA VERGINE DI SAN LUCA
6	GIARDINI MARGHERITA	18	ARCO DEL MELONCELLO
7	PORTA CASTIGLIONE	19	TEATRO DELLE CELEBRAZIONI
8	CHIESA DI S.MARIA DELLA MISERICORDIA	20	PORTA S. ISAIA
9	PORTA SAN MAMOLO	21	PORTA SAN FELICE BI-20.mp3
10	CHIESA DI SAN MICHELE IN BOSCO	22	PORTA LAME
11	PARCO DI SAN MICHELE IN BOSCO		
12	CHIESA DI S.PAOLO IN MONTE ALL'OSSERVANZA		

Tappe del percorso

Tappe del percorso
con Audioguida

Nome del file audio

Given the length of this tour, it is recommended to travel by public transportation or private means of transport, even though you must consider the parking difficulties you will experience along the ring avenues.

Keep the city's centre on your right and start from the

PORTA MASCARELLA

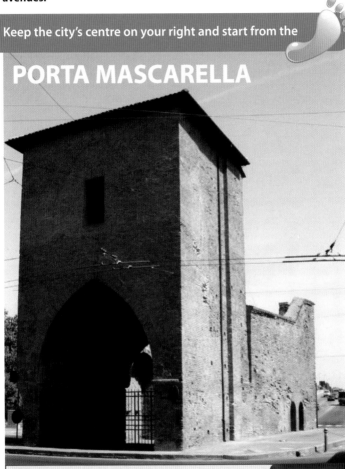

line n. 32, 33 (P.ta Mascarella)

UTILITY

The door belongs to the third and last circle of the walls dating back to the second half of the 13th century. Visitors can see the remains of the original construction that was then remodelled and lowered during the 16th century. It was isolated at the beginning of the 20th century as a consequence of the demolition of the walls.

Continue along the avenues until you reach the

PORTA ZAMBONI
(formerly Porta San Donato)

🚌 line n. 20,28,32, 33, 36,37, 89, 93, 94, 99 (P.ta S.Donato)　UTILITY

This door too belongs to the third and last circle of the walls dating back to the second half of the 13th century.

It was transformed in the 15th century and still holds the ancient forepart or ravelin.

Continue along the avenues until you reach the

PORTA SAN VITALE

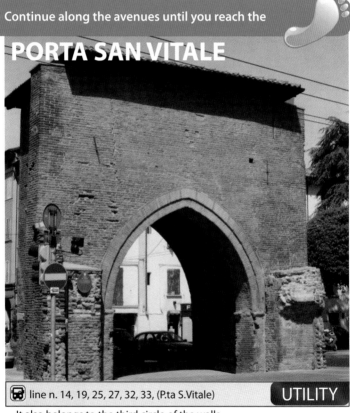

line n. 14, 19, 25, 27, 32, 33, (P.ta S.Vitale)   UTILITY

It also belongs to the third circle of the walls.

It was erected in 1286 and was surmounted by an ancient tower demolished in the 14th century. It was protected by a revelin situated across the moat and originally preceded by a drawbridge, that was installed in 1354 and eliminated at the end of the 18th century. The forepart was destroyed in 1952.

Continue along the avenues until you reach the

PORTA DI STRADA MAGGIORE (MAZZINI)

line n. 14, 19, 25, 27, 32, 33 (P.ta Mazzini)   UTILITY

It belongs to the third and last circle of the walls dating back to the second half of the 13th century. It was redesigned by Gian Giacomo Dotti in 1770 and reduced to its current appearance, on the basis of the remains found after the demolition carried out at the beginning of the 20th century.

realign the mouths of the roads meeting there, it was necessary to create a new opening into the walls. Over the following decades, the comprehensive realignment was carried out and a new long bridge over the moat was built.

In 1903 the destruction of the door was decided on. However, once the demolition had already started and after a long and lively debate, in 1909 there prevailed the opinion of those who wanted to hold and renovate the remained ruins, which belonged to the most ancient construction.

Continue along the avenues until you reach the

PORTA SANTO STEFANO

line n. 16, 32, 33, 38, 39 (P.ta S.Stefano)

UTILITY

Over the course of many centuries, through this door, of which nothing remains today, princes, popes and King Victor Emmanuel II coming from Rome or Florence entered the city.

The current buildings that replace the medieval door were erected in 1843 by the architect Filippo Antolini at the request of Pope Gregory XVI.

LE PRIME
UNITÀ DEL NUOVO ESERCITO ITALIANO
ENTRARONO
IN BOLOGNA RESTITUITA ALLA LIBERTÀ
IL 21 APRILE 1945

LA CITTÀ VUOLE QUI RICORDATI
CON GRATITUDINE ED ONORE
I FANTI DELL' 87° REGGIMENTO
DEL GRUPPO DI COMBATTIMENTO 'FRIULI'
I BERSAGLIERI E GLI ARDITI
DEL GRUPPO DI COMBATTIMENTO 'LEGNANO'
I PARACADUTISTI
DEL GRUPPO DI COMBATTIMENTO 'FOLGORE'

A CURIOUS NOTE

The toll barrier was closed by means of a gate that was then transferred to the entrance to the Giardini Margherita, next to the Porta Castiglione, where it is still today.

GIARDINI MARGHERITA

Viale Gozzadini   UTILITY

line n. 16, 32, 33, 38, 39 (P.Castiglione) (Giardini Margherita)

good

This is the main public park of Bologna.

In 1874, the Municipality of Bologna acquired a plot of land located along the last walls between Porta Castiglione and Porta Santo Stefano, in order to create there a public park. The design was entrusted to Count Sambuy, who personally supervised the realization of his design that was executed by the engineer Tubertini.

In 1879 it was decided to name the park after "Her Majesty Queen Margaret", who had visited the city the previous year, so the Bologna's citizens got used to calling it "*Giardini Margherita*" ("*Margaret's park*").

The inauguration took place on July 6th 1879, and from that date onwards the Park has been the venue for a large number of events and manifestations marking the Bologna's life.

During the construction works a large Etruscan necropolis was discovered. It was very rich in finds, which today are housed in the Bologna's Museo Civico Archeologico. Later, two of the recovered tombs were reconstructed inside the park.

At one of the main entrances there is the equestrian monument to Victor Emmanuel II, dating back to 1945.

Inside visitors can find linden trees, oaks, yews, cedars, plane trees, pine trees, horse chestnut trees, magnolias, which follow a course of main paths and walkways.

An especially impressive path is the one of the pond, that has been created with waters of Savena river and is provided with a chalet, a small bridge, an artificial island, as well as aquatic flora and fauna.

In the early 20th century an outdoor school was built, which still exists.

In the main small square of the park there is a little building that for several years the Municipality used as Library for Young People.

During the sixties a group of amateur astronomers, authorized by the Municipality, built an astronomical observatory on the terrace, which is still functioning.

Over the time there were held Exhibitions, Performances, Horse shows, Concerts and Motor races. In 1988, the helicopter transporting Pope John Paul II to Bologna landed there. On that occasion the Pope visited the University of Bologna to celebrate the ninth centenary of its foundation.

A CURIOUS NOTE

The equestrian monument to Victor Emmanuel II was inaugurated in Bologna in 1880.

Originally, it embellished the "Crescentone" in Piazza Maggiore (this is the name with which the Bologna's citizens like to call the huge step placed at the centre of the square), when the square was still called Piazza Vittorio Emanuele.

At the end of the Second World War, in 1945, the monument was moved to the Giardini Margherita, where it still stands.

Continue along the avenues until you reach the

PORTA CASTIGLIONE

line n. 16, 32, 33, 38, 39 (P.ta S.Stefano)   UTILITY

This door belongs to the third and last circle of the walls dating back to the second half of the 13th century.

It was remodelled at the beginning of the 15th century, while in the first years of the 20th century, as a consequence of the demolition of the walls, it assumed its current appearance.

Porta Castiglione could be named "Door of canals", since nearby the Savena canal entered the city.

Through its branches it supplied many tens of medieval factories processing wool and silk with hydraulic energy and the corresponding driving force.

Immediately outside the door, close to one of the exits of the Giardini Margherita, you will find the

CHIESA DI SANTA MARIA DELLA MISERICORDIA

(icon) **piazza porta Castiglione, 4**	UTILITY

(icon) +39.051.332.755 (icon) Working days 7.30-11.30 and 16.30-20
Holidays 8.30-13 and 16-20 (icon) line n. 16, 30, 38, 39, 59, A (P.Castiglione)

The current church was built by the Olivetan friars in 1432.

The façade holds traces of the Romanesque church dating back to the period in which it belonged to the Cistercian nuns.

The portico, dating back to the end of the 15th century, was later enlarged.

Inside visitors can admire paintings by Lippo di Dalmasio, Bagnacavallo, B. Cesi, Spisanelli, U. Gandolfi (1777), stained-glass windows by F. Francia (1499) and a peculiar wooden tabernacle by Matteo Cossich called "il Tedesco" (1624).

A CURIOUS NOTE

The Congregazione di Monte Oliveto Maggiore drew its origin from some Sienese nobles: Bernardo Tolomei (1272-1348), Patrizio Patrizi and Ambrogio Piccolomini, who in 1313 retired to a solitary place called Accona, later Monte Oliveto, located about thirty kilometres away from Siena. They desired to establish "a school of divine service" (Rule of Saint Benedict), and received the white monastic dress by the vicar of the bishop of Arezzo by professing the Rule of Saint Benedict.

The Blessed Bernardo Tolomei crowned his life with a touching and charitable act of heroism. Actually he died, together with other eighty of his brother monks, while nursing the plague victims in Siena during the plague of 1348.

The 15th century was a golden period for the Olivetan friars, the followers of the Blessed Bernardo were more than 900 and had 53 monasteries. Also this Congregation suffered persecutions from several governments, with suppressions and expropriations.

Continue along the avenues until you reach the

PORTA SAN MAMOLO

This door, located immediately after the exit from Via d'Azeglio at the crossing of Viale Panzacchi, Viale Aldini and Via di Porta S. Mamolo, does not exist any more.

A CURIOUS NOTE

Porta San Mamolo is one of the doors that do not exist any more because they were demolished with the walls in 1903.

It was built in the 12th century and renovated many times, in 1334 it was equipped with a drawbridge over the external moat. In 1417 a new *cassero* was erected.

In 1850 the whole structure underwent a renovation work, however this was useless to stop the destructive fury of the "progressives".

On April 15th 1903, the City's Council voted the decision to demolish the Porta S. Mamolo (or d'Azeglio), since it held up the traffic and prevented the construction works of the electric tram line from being continued.

Exit the door and take Via S.Mamolo, then turn left to the second side street, Via Codivilla. Continue straight until you reach the large square, the turn right and go up the slope of Saint Benedict, that leads in front of the

CHIESA DI SAN MICHELE IN BOSCO

UTILITY

📍 **Piazzale San Michele in Bosco, 3**

☎ +39.051.636.63.28

🕐 Working days 9-12 and 16-19

♿ very limited

🚌 line n. 30 (S.Michele Bosco)

This is an imposing architectural complex consisting of the church and the adjacent former Olivetan monastery. It stands on one of the more panoramic spots of the hills located near Bologna, and its courtyard is a splendid balcony over the city and the plain up to the Alpine chain.

The church has ancient origins; actually it was erected during the Middle Ages, and between 1517 and 1523 it was rebuilt in its current appearance by the Olivetan monks, who had settled there ever since 1364.

The Renaissance harmonious facade was executed by Biagio Rossetti from Ferrara, while the really fine marble portal is a work by Baldassarre Peruzzi (1522).

The interior features a single nave, with four chapels and a large presbytery closed by two barriers. On the right side of the presbytery two doors open. The first one leads to the long corridor of the ancient monastery, also known as *"il Cannocchiale"* ("the Telescope") because, thanks to an optical effect, it seems as if you can touch the Torre degli Asinelli. The second door leads to the valuable Cloister called "dei Carracci", the walls of which are decorated with the very famous *frescoes* by Ludovico Carracci and other Bologna's painters, among whom is Guido Reni. Of great interest are also the sacristy and the night choir featuring 16th century frescoes.

A CURIOUS NOTE

The first stone of the church was laid down by Pope Eugenius IV in 1437. Ten years later, in 1447, it was seemingly already finished, since Giovanni Poggi was consecrated Bishop of Bologna right there.

From this view you can see the

PARCO DI SAN MICHELE IN BOSCO

 line n. 29, 52 (Annunziata) 30 (P.le Bacchelli)
 5.30-23

UTILITY

The hill of San Michele in Bosco has a very ancient history. Initially it housed a cenoby of hermits who had taken refuge there, afterwards, during the 14th century, the Monastery was erected. Over the century, it was embellished and enlarged many times. Towards the middle of the 16th century, the Monastery reached its maximum splendour thanks to the execution of the cloister by Carraccis and the reconstruction of the church, attributed to the urbanist and architect Biagio Rossetti from Ferrara. From the balcony on which the complex stands, you can enjoy a marvellous view over the city.

Since 1895 the Monastery has become the seat of the Istituto Ortopedico Rizzoli. The Olivetan friars came back in 1933 and some of them still live in a part of the Monastery itself.

The park was created at the end of the 19th century, when the Monastery became a hospital. It stretches from the church on the hillside, and descends towards Via Codivilla through a long winding road.

The vegetation is almost exclusively arboreal. In the Western side, the vegetation is more varied and, together with centuries old oaks, it includes ornamental trees many of which date back to the epoch of the establishment of the park: monumental holm oaks, cypress-trees, lime-trees, horse chestnut trees and cedars.

The Parco di San Michele in Bosco, which in the down part facing Via Codivilla is called Giardino Remo Scoto, belongs to the Istituto Ortopedico Rizzoli.

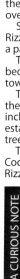

A CURIOUS NOTE

The strategic position of the Monastero di S. Michele in Bosco, namely a large "balcony" looking out to Bologna, made it often a subject of dispute. The military invasions suffered forced the friars to abandon the monastery and take refuge inside the city.

Following the Napoleon's suppression of the monastery and the expulsion of Benedictine friars in 1797, the whole complex was initially transformed into a shelter for soldiers, then it became a place of punishment (1804).

The restoration taking place after the fall of Napoleon gave Bologna back to the Holy See and returned the monastery to the Bologna's Church. Again, the strategic position and the panoramic view over the city took the Papal Legate, Cardinal Spinola (1843), to choose it as summer residence after renovating and adjusting it for the required purpose.

Also the Austrians appreciated its position, and in 1849, during the Risorgimento riots, they used this place to better bomb the rebel city.

Upon the unification of Italy occurred through a revolutionary action in 1859, the moderates took the upper hand, thus allowing Bologna to be included in the constitutional monarchy of the Reign of Sardinia. During that period the sovereigns of Savoia house used the place as Royal villa (1860). Since 1896 it has been the seat of the very famous Istituto Rizzoli, following the wish of the outstanding surgeon Francesco Rizzoli.

Turn back and go on until you reach Via S. Mamolo (outside the door) again, then turn right and immediately take the ascending road on the left, Via dell'Osservanza, continue straight ahead until number 88, where you will find the

CHIESA DI SAN PAOLO IN MONTE ALL'OSSERVANZA

✠ **via dell'Osservanza, 88**   UTILITY

🕐 Opening hours: during Holy Masses.

Museo Missionario d'Arte Cinese and Museo dell'Osservanza: inside the Monastery of the friars minor of Observance ☎ +39.051.580597

🕐 only by appointment (preferably in the afternoon) 🚌 line n. 52 (Osservanza)

The church has a monastery of the Observant Friars Minor.

It is located on the top of a hill, where a small church dedicated to Saint Paul stood. Nearby there is a cave where, according to a documented tradition, Saint Anthony retired to meditate during his teaching of theology in Bologna in the years 1223-27.

In 1407 the Observant Friars Minor were donated the amount of money required to build the church and the monastery and, on December 9th 1409, Pope Alexander V granted them full power to do so. On December 23rd 1417 the work was finished.

The complex of the Observance suffered the Napoleon's suppression. Afterwards the church was bought by the lawyer Antonio Aldini, a deputy of the Cisalpine Republic, in order to build a villa for Napoleon's stays in Bologna (which never occurred).

In 1824, the other parts of the complex were bought by a devout woman from Bologna, who then donated it to the Friars Minor, thus allowing them to take possession of it again.

In 1828 it was completely rebuilt by Vincenzo Vannini in neoclassical style.

The interior houses paintings by artists belonging to Bologna's school, such as: G. Gatti, C. Cignani, E. Sirani, B. Burrini, Orazio di Jacopo, and sculptures by F. Scandellari.

In the sacristy visitors can admire paintings by O. Samacchini, G.F. Gessi, N. Bertuzzi, L. Crespi, A. Magnoni, while the refectory holds works by L. Tadolini, A. and L. Crespi, J. A. Calvi, G. and U. Gandolfi, G. Varotti, G. Pedretti.

Within its walls the cave of Saint Anthony can still be seen.

Turn back and reach number 35, there you will see the

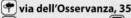
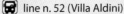

VILLA ALDINI

✠ **via dell'Osservanza, 35**   **UTILITY**

☎ +39.051.581444   🚌 line n. 52 (Villa Aldini)

It was designed by Giuseppe Nadi and dates back to 1816. In the building Ionic order was used, and it features eight columns sitting on an elevated surface; in the tympanum visitors can admire a stucco bas-relief by G. De Maria.

This villa is told to have been erected by Antonio Aldini (who was a minister of Napoleon) in order to give hospitality to the Emperor that, when he came to Bologna, had appreciated the splendid view over the city being enjoyed from that spot of Via dell'Osservanza. Maybe this is only a legend, in any case Napoleon had no occasion to be lodged there.

Following the fall of Napoleon and the ruin of Aldini, the villa was abandoned, while its decoration was never completed. Moreover, it was never employed for its intended use.

After the renovation work carried out by Guido Zucchini in 1939, in the back of the building visitors can see the last remains of the very ancient round church dedicated to Saint Mary of the Mount, which was a hermitage for women. Actually, that small church was demolished to build the Villa Aldini.

A CURIOUS NOTE

If the building still exists today, we must say thanks to the presence of the Rotonda della Madonna del Monte inside it. Originally, this was a Sanctuary, then it was embedded in the new neoclassical building and transformed into dining hall.

In 1831, a private citizen bought the whole building for only 3.600 *scudis* with the intention of using it as building material. However, the "Pia Unione dei Devoti della Madonna del Monte", with the support of the Municipality of Bologna, managed to acquire the building back for 6.530 scudis in order to devote it to religious worship.

PORTA SARAGOZZA

Museo della Beata Vergine di San Luca:

UTILITY

🕆 **Piazza di Porta Saragozza, 2/a** ☎ +39.051.6447421

🕐 Tue-Sat 9-13; Thursday 9-18; Sunday 10-18   ℹ free

🚌 line n. 20, 32, 33, 38, 39,94, D (P.ta Saragozza)

It was erected in 1860 on the remains of the medieval walls.

It was designed by Enrico Brunetti Rodati.

This door was built between two large towers with battlements on top. Between the two towers there are three arches, and one of the towers holds the "*Cassero*", which features a beautiful terrace that is open during the summer.

A CURIOUS NOTE

Considering the vicissitudes the Porta Saragozza underwent especially from the 17th century onwards, it could be called the "Door of pilgrims", and not only because through it believers passed to reach the top of the Colle della Guardia and venerate the icon of the Blessed Virgin of Saint Luke, but also because its name - probably originating from a mythical victory of the Christian armies against Muslims – evoked the far away West of the pilgrimages to the Iberian land.

It was built in the 13th century, and in 1334 it was equipped with a forepart and a drawbridge over the moat. Today it has the appearance it was given by the radical renovation carried out by the architect Giuseppe Mengoni in 1859. He replaced the medieval cassero by the current one, and linked it to the two side cylindrical towers through two battlemented porticos.

For long it remained a secondary passage, and often it was not used. It gained special importance from when, in 1674, the long portico leading to the Basilica della B. V. di San Luca was erected, thus it became the point of arrival and departure of the processions accompanying the icon of Mary, that before passed through the Porta di Sant'Isaia.

In front of the door there starts the

PORTICO DI SAN LUCA

Via San Luca

line n. 20, 32, 33, 38, 39,94, D (P.ta Saragozza)

UTILITY

The idea of building an arcade connecting the city with the top of the hill dates back to 1655, however it could only be started 20 years later.

It was designed by the architect Giovanni Giacomo Monti and it seems that then the whole city of Bologna had contributed to

the expenses for its construction.

The portico consists of 666 arches financed by the religious congregations, the noble families and the associations of citizens from all social classes. Those who could not give money donations supplied building material or worked personally.

Each arch is numbered and between the arches 132 and 133 a plaque commemorating the laying of the first stone was placed.

It is greatly loved by Bologna's citizens, that use it to go on a pilgrimage to the mount.

It is 4 kilometres long and features an inclination of about 200 metres.

The Madonna di San Luca started to be venerated by all Bologna's citizens when the statue was carried to the city to pray for the end of a period of bad weather.

Every year since then the statue is carried to the city through the arcade and, as mentioned above, the Bologna's citizens walk on a pilgrimage through the arcade up to the mount.

During the descent you can admire the view over the city's northwest side, and see from above the Stadio Comunale and the Palazzetto dello Sport.

Take Via Saragozza towards the out-of-town area. After about two kilometres, on your left you will find the

VILLA SPADA

🛉 **via di Casaglia 3** **UTILITY**

Museo Storico Didattico della Tappezzeria: ☎ +39.051.6145512

🕐 Tue-Sun 9-13 Closed: Monday, midweek Holydays, Christmas, New Year's Day, May 1st ⓘ 4/2 € 🚌 line n. 20 (Villa Spada) ♿ good

It is located in Via Saragozza at the corner with Via Casaglia, in the city's area placed at the foot of the hills, and it features one of the more popular parks in Bologna and Saragozza district.

The building was erected in the 18th century following the wish of Jacopo Zambettari, who entrusted the architect Giovanni Battista Martinetti with its construction. This same architect also designed the Italian-style park, used as a link with the surrounding park that already existed.

In 1820 the property was handed over to the *Marchesa* Beaufort, who was married with the Roman prince Clemente Spada Veralli. He completed the complex by annexing the area currently placed along Via Saragozza to the park.

In 1849, it became the seat of the Austrian general headquarters, afterwards other owners succeeded one another until when, during the sixties, the villa and the park were acquired by the Municipality of Bologna and then opened to public.

Since 1984 the villa houses the Museo della Tappezzeria, and today it is also the seat of the library of Saragozza district.

In the afternoon of August 5th 1849, two prisoners started their transfer from Cesenatico, where the followers of Garibaldi had been intercepted while being in a disorderly retreat, firstly to Ravenna and then to Bologna. There they were waited for in the Austrian general headquarters, located in the Villa Spada.

The escort consisted of 50 Austrian soldiers and was proportional to the prisoners' value. In the evening of August 7th, the two prisoners were locked up in the medieval turret placed in the park of the villa.

Without bringing any judicial action, General Gorzkowski accused the Barnabite Father Ugo Bassi, chaplain of the Garibaldi's legion, of possession of arms and Giovanni Livraghi of desertion. The penalty imposed was the immediate execution by shooting, so as to give a warning to all Bologna's citizens, and it happened before the curia could put the Barnabite Father Ugo Bassi under the protection of canon law. In the morning of August 8th the sentence was executed.

If you are travelling by car, you can reach the Santuario di S. Luca from Via Casaglia. If you are travelling by BUS, at the Villa Spada stop take the minibus Cosepuri that will bring you to the

SANTUARIO DELLA BEATA VERGINE DI SAN LUCA

✠ **Via di S. Luca, 36** ☎ +39.051.6142339   UTILITY

🕐 7-12.30 afternoon from October to February 14.30-17, March 14.30-18, other months 14.30-19. On summer days 12.30-14.30. During the church services, the sightseeing could be limited or suspended. The hours are subject to slight changes ♿ very limited 🚌 line n. 20 , go down at the stop Villa Spada and take the private minibus Cosepuri

Tradition tells us that the Grecian pilgrim Teocle Kmnega received the image of the Virgin painted by the Evangelist Luke from the canons of the church of Saint Sophia in Constantinople, with the commission to bring it to the Monte della Guardia.

When he came to Rome he learnt that the mount was in Bologna, so the image reached that city in 1160.

The sanctuary, designed by Carlo Francesco Dotti, was built in the 18th century as a tribute to that image of the "Virgin and Child", and was called the *Madonna di S. Luca* since it is traditionally attributed to the apostle Luke.

It is also believed that the image represents a Byzantine painting probably dating back no earlier than the 12th century, that was formerly in possession of two young girls, Azolina and Bice, daughters of Rambertino. Apparently, they erected in 1160 a small hermitage on the Colle della Guardia to hold this venerated image.

A CURIOUS NOTE

In 1433 the Bologna's people carried the Madonna in a procession in order to implore for the end of violent rains, which were destroying the harvests, thus creating the condition for a famine period.

When they came to Porta Saragozza the rain stopped and, in thanksgiving, the Elders ordered that the procession had to be repeated every year, and this still occurs today.

184

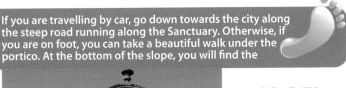

If you are travelling by car, go down towards the city along the steep road running along the Sanctuary. Otherwise, if you are on foot, you can take a beautiful walk under the portico. At the bottom of the slope, you will find the

ARCO DEL MELONCELLO

It was designed by Dotti with a probable intervention of the scene-painter Francesco Bibiena.

This aedicule featuring a curvilinear plan and using the free column is, together with the area in front of the basilica, the only outside Baroque space in the city.

 Via Saragozza   line n. 20, 94 (Meloncello)   UTILITY

If you are on foot take Via Saragozza towards the city's centre, and after about 200 metres on your right you will find the Teatro delle Celebrazioni. If you are by car, park it because you are forced to go towards the stadium, after the Arco del Meloncello.

TEATRO DELLE CELEBRAZIONI

Via Saragozza, 234

 +39.051.6176111   line n. 20, 94 (Meloncello)

It belongs to the complex of the "*Casa di riposo Lyda Borelli per artisti drammatici*" (Lyda Borelli nursing home for dramatic artists).

It was built in 1950 and renovated in 1997. The hall contains 998 seats.

The stage measures 26 metres in width and 3.50 metres in depth, while the proscenium measures 16 metres in width and 9 metres in height.

If you are by BUS, take it and go towards the avenues, then continue the tour interrupted at Porta Saragozza. If you are by car, go ahead alongside the stadium until you cross Via Andrea Costa, then turn right and follow this road until the end, until you reach the ring avenues near Porta Sant'Isaia (that also does not exist any more) and turn left

PORTA S. ISAIA

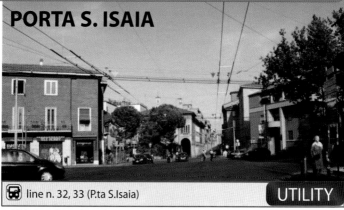

line n. 32, 33 (P.ta S.Isaia)

This is a door that does not exist any more, and is located immediately after the exit from Via Sant'Isaia at the corner with Viale G.Vinci, Viale C.Pepoli and Via Andrea Costa.

A CURIOUS NOTE

Porta Sant'Isaia is one of the doors that do not exist any more since they were demolished with the walls in 1903.

On June 15th of that year, the city council voted for the demolition of Porta Sant'Isaia (formerly Porta Pia), since it was deemed not very stable.

PORTA SAN FELICE

line n. 13, 19, 32, 33, 36, 38, 39 (P.ta S.Felice)   **UTILITY**

It is located at the crossroads of Via S. Felice, Via Saffi, Viale Vicini and Viale Silvani.

It stands exactly in front of the road leading to Modena (Via Saffi/Emilia Ponente).

Actually this door represented the access to the city for those who came from Modena and generally from the North, and through Via San Felice it led directly to the heart of the city.

A CURIOUS NOTE

Through this door there passed the armies going towards the West, and also King Enzo entered the city by passing through it after he was taken prisoner. Moreover, in 1325 the troops from Modena, after having defeated the Bologna's army in battle, stopped in front of the door and, as a scornful gesture, took the bucket of a nearby well, namely the "kidnapped bucket".

It had a strategic importance thanks to its position on the Via Emilia.

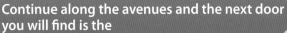

Continue along the avenues and the next door you will find is the

PORTA LAME

🚌 line n. 18, 32, 33, 35, B (P.ta Lame)

UTILITY

This door was designed by Agostino Barelli and built in 1677. It belongs to the third and last circle of the walls.

The bronze statues representing young partisans executed by Luciano Minguzzi commemorate a battle that took place near the door on November 7th 1944.

A CURIOUS NOTE

Porta delle Lame could be called "Door of waters" due to both the nearness to the port and the adjacent Salara (i.e., a warehouse for salt), and the road passing through the door itself and leading to several stretches of water that covered the Bologna's low plain (in Latin "lama" means pond, marsh).

It was built in the 13th century with a covered cassero; in 1334 it was equipped with two drawbridges: one for wagons and the other for pedestrians. It was repeatedly closed due to the difficulty to defend it. Between 1674 and 1677, it was radically renovated through the demolition of the medieval cassero and the construction of the current building in Baroque style.

Here is the virtual end of this tour.

USEFUL INFORMATION

ARRIVALS:

Guglielmo Marconi airport - www.bologna-airport.it - Tel. 051/647.96.15
It is connected to the city centre:

Shuttle service- **AEROBUS - BLQ**
The Aerobus line - BLQ is the service directly connecting the Bologna's Guglielmo
Marconi airport with the city centre and the Railway Station.On the occasion
of the main exhibitions, the direct connection Airport – Fiera District is active.
The ticket can also be purchased on board.
For more information Tel. 051 290.290.

TAXI
Radio Taxi C.A.T. – Consorzio Autonomo Tassisti
(Independent Association of Taxi Drivers) – Tel, 051 234 141
Cotabo – Cooperativa Taxista Bolognesi – (Bologna's Cooperative of Taxi Drivers)
Tel. 051 372.727.

CAR HIRE WITH DRIVER
CAB – Tel 39 051 553.415 - *Car Hire with Driver*

CAR RENTAL COMPANIES AT THE AIRPORT

AVIS –	Tel. 051 – 647.20.32
HERTZ -	Tel. 051 647.20.15
EUROPCAR -	Tel. 051 – 647.21.11
MAGGIORE -	Tel. 051 – 647.20.07
SIXT -	Tel. 051 547.20.27
SICILY BY CAR – AUTOEUROPA -	Tel. 051 647.20.06
THRIFTY -	Tel. 051 647.20.22
AUTOVIA -	Tel. 051 647.24.52

*The parking spaces reserved to the Car Rental companies are located at level **1** of*
*(multi-level) parking **P2**, there clients can collect the car (and return it at the end of*
the hire period)

STATE BODIES AT THE AIRPORT

A.C.I. Breakdown Service	Tel. 051.80.31.16
Carabinieri	Tel. 051 647.93.00
State Corps of Forest Rangers	Tel. 051 313.448
Customs office	Tel. 051 647.93.48
National Society for Flight Assistance	Tel. 051 413.91.28
National Body of Civil Aviation	Tel. 051 647.96.90
Finance Police	Tel. 051 647.93.34
Frontier Police	Tel. 051 542.19.11
Municipal Police	Tel. 051 647.93.71
Emergency aid facility	Tel. 051 647.97.90
Air health service	Tel. 051 385.995
Veterinary service	Tel. 051 647.21.55
Fire service	Tel. 051 402.094

TRAIN

The railway station is very close to the city centre. Tel 848.888.088

BUS STATION

It is close to the Railway Station. Tel. 051.29.02.92

CAR

PUBLIC PARKING AREAS in Bologna, with opening hours and interchange opportunities

Key:

PARK + BUS: **interchange with bus:** FREE parking for ATC users

PARK + TRAIN: **interchange with train:** parking area near the railway station

PARK + TAXI: **interchange with taxi:** FREE parking for TAXI users

PARK + BICI: **interchange with bicycle:** FREE parking for those who deposit their bikes and use them after parking the car

PARK + C'entro in Bici: **interchange with bicycle "C'entro in bici":** parking with the possibility of collecting a bike having a personalized key

TANARI PARKING (via Tanari); PARK + BUS + TRAIN + BIKE + TAXI + C'entro in Bici; BUS: line 18, 35, shuttles A (FS main railway station) and B; 400 spaces – guarded; Hours: 0 - 24.00 (all days)

PRATI DI CAPRARA PARKING (Via Prati di Caprara - Via Emilia Ponente); PARK + BUS + BIKE + TAXI; BUS: lines 13 - 19 - 35 - 38 - 39 - 81 - 86 - 87 - 91 - 92 – 93; 180 spaces – guarded; Hours: 07.00 - 21.00 (closed on holidays)

GIURIOLO PARKING (via Giuriolo); PARK + BUS + BIKE; BUS: lines 11 - 27 - 95 - 97 -98 ; 500 spaces – guarded; Hours: 07.00 - 21.00 (August and holidays excluded)

LARGO LERCARO (via Lercaro); PARK + C'entro in Bici; BUS: 11 - 36 - 38 - 39 – 51; 240 spaces – not guarded – free; Hours: 0 - 24.00 (all days); Every Wednesday morning the street market takes place there

ANTISTADIO (via Andrea Costa); PARK + BUS + BIKE + C'entro in Bici; BUS: lines 14 - 21 – 89; 283 spaces – remote controlled; Hours: 07.00 - 21.00 (August and holidays excluded)

S.ORSOLA - MALPIGHI (via Albertoni); PARK + C'entro in Bici; BUS: lines 14 - 19 - 25 - 27 - 36 - 60 - 89 - 94 – 99; 450 spaces – guarded; Hours: 0 - 24.00 (06 -22 with personnel present / 22-06 with remote control) - (all days)

FIORAVANTI PARKING(via Fioravanti); 190 spaces – guarded; working days 6.30 - 22 (holidays excluded)

VIII Agosto PARKING(Piazza VIII Agosto); BUS: lines 11 - 20 - 27 - 28 - 36 - 37 - 89 - 93 - 94 - 99 - A – C; 700 spaces – guarded; Hours: 0 - 24.00 (all days)

Ex Staveco PARKING (viale Panzacchi); PARK + C'entro in Bici; BUS: lines 32, 33, 59, shuttles A – E; 180 spaces – guarded; Hours: 07.30 - 01.00 (all days)

Zaccherini Alvisi PARKING (via Zaccherini Alvisi);PARK + Free rental of bicycles (for those using the fee parking); BUS: lines 14,36, 89, 99; 500 spaces – guarded; Hours: 0 - 24.00 (all days)

Sferisterio - Piazzale Baldi PARKING (via Irnerio); BUS: ines 11 - 20 - 27 - 28 - 36 - 37 - 89 - 93 - 94 - 99 - A – C; 74 spaces – remote controlled; Hours 0 - 24.00 (excluded: Friday and Saturday from 5.30 to 20.30 and special market days)

Certosa PARKING (Viale Gandhi) (parking on Stadio area); PARK + C'entro in Bici; 325 posti

Piazza della Pace PARKING (Piazza della Pace) (parking on Stadio area); 291 spaces
Ghisello PARKING (Via della Barca) (parcheggio zona Stadio); <u>PARK + C'entro in Bici</u>; 115 posti
Manifattura Tabacchi PARKING (via della Manifattura)
(parking on Fair district); 253 spaces, only open on fair days
   Parco Nord PARKING (via Stalingrado) (parking
on Fair district); 750 spaces - only open on fair days
Piazza Costituzione PARKING (Piazza Costituzione)
(parking on Fair district); 369 spaces - only open on fair days
Michelino PARKING (Viale Europa) (parking on Fair district); 3270 spaces - only open on fair days

MOVING AROUND in BOLOGNA

Hourly Ticket for city area, € 1.00: it allows you to travel by any ATC transportation of Bologna's city network with the exception of Aerobus. <u>Ticket validity:</u> it must be stamped at the beginning of the journey. It can be used in the whole city area of Bologna and is valid for **60 minutes** from the moment it is stamped on board. It is valid for **70 minutes from 20.30 to 6.30.** It is valid for **90 minutes** during summer when the short hours of August are in use.

Daily Ticket: it allows you to travel by any ATC transportation of Bologna's city network, and to use several lines, with the exception of Aerobus. <u>Ticket validity:</u> it must be stamped at the beginning of the journey. It can be used in the whole city area of Bologna and is valid for **24 hours** from the moment it is stamped on board.

CITY PASS 10 journeys**: this is a not-individual and transferable ticket**. It can be used by one or more persons at the same time and must be stamped once for each user. **It allows you to travel** on any route of the city areas in which you have stamped the ticket, and to use several lines during the validity period. It allows you to travel in one of the city areas of: Bologna, Imola, Castel S. Pietro Terme, Porretta Terme, with the exception of Aerobus. <u>Ticket validity:</u> it is valid for 10 journeys no longer than 60 minutes from the moment it is stamped on board. It is valid for 70 minutes from 20.30 to 6.30. It is valid for 90 minutes during summer when the short hours of August are in use.

ECO Days: **Also** perfect for people going shopping in the city centre, families, tourists and groups. **This is a not-individual and transferable ticket**. It can be used by one or more persons at the same time, and must be stamped once for each user at the beginning of the first journey. <u>Ticket validity:</u> It allows you to travel for 11 days, not necessarily in a row. Each stamping enables you to travel for the next 24 hours by any transportation in the Bologna's city area, including the route of the Bologna - Vignola Suburban Railway

INFORMATION IN SITU

I.A.T. Informazione Assistenza Turistica (Tourist Assistance Information) – G. Marconi Airport – Arrivals Hall – Via Triunvirato 84 – All days 9.00 – 19.00 – December 31st 9.00 – 17.00 Closed: New Year's Day, Easter, Christmas Day and Saint Stephen's Day.

Public Toilets

Almost all coffee bars and cafeterias have public toilets. However, before using them, it is recommended to take something, even a simple glass of water.

Tip

In most restaurants you will find the "service" item at the bottom of the menu. However, if you are unsure, ask the waiter if prices include service. If you want, you can round the bill up, without feeling uncomfortable.

EMERGENCY SERVICES

First Aid	Tel. 118
Police	Tel. 113
Carabinieri	Tel. 112
Finance Police	Tel. 117
Municipal Police (rapid intervention)	Tel. 051/26.66.26
Fire service	Tel. 115
Traffic Police	Tel. 051/52.69.11
Physicians on duty	Tel. 848.831.831 (districts of Borgo Panigale, Reno, Saragozza, Porto and Navile)
	Tel. 848.832.832 (districts of San Vitale, San Donato, Santo Stefano and Savena)
Dentists on duty	Tel. 051/54.38.50
Obstetricians on duty	Tel. 051/636.44.29
Antivenin Centre	Tel. 051/647.89.55
C.R.I. Italian Red Cross	Tel. 051/23.45.67
Medicine first aid	Tel. 800.218.489 (home delivery of urgent medicines)
Chemists on duty	Tel. 800.21.84.89 (medicine service)
	Tel. 800.54.74.54 (health service)
A.N.T. (National association for cancer research)	Tel. 051/38.31.31

FOUND OBJECTS OFFICE

Via dell'Industria, 2 – Tel. 051 601.86.26; *Opening hours:* From Monday To Friday, from 8.00 to 13.00; Tuesday and Thursday from 14.30 to 17.00 – closed: Saturday

LOSS of the CREDIT CARD

In case of loss or theft of your Credit Card, it is advisable to immediately inform the Customer Service Centre about it in order to **block the Card**. In the following table you will find some of the main telephone numbers to be called in case of loss or theft of your credit card:

Agos Itafinco	Tel. 800 82.20.56
American Express	Tel. 800 86.40.46
Banca Finem	Tel. 800 52.52.52

Banca Sella	Tel. 800 82.20.56
Barclaycard	Tel. 800 90.80.69
Carta Si	Tel. 800 15.16.16
Citybank	Tel. 800 40.77.04
Deutschebank	Tel. 800 20.71.67
Diner's	Tel. 800 86.40.64
Findomestic	Tel. 800 86.61.16
Servizi Interbancari	Tel. 800 15.16.16
Top Card	Tel. 800 90.09.10
Visa	Tel. 800 15.16.16

Musei e Collezioni* / *Museums and Collections * / *museos y colecciones

Collezione D'Arte Rolo Banca (Unicredito) - Via Zamboni, 20 - Tel.:051 2962508
Collezione Opera Pia dei Poveri Vergognosi - Via Marsala, 7 - Tel.: 051 2966211
Collezione Storica Atc - Via Bigari, 1/a - Tel.: 051 379006
MAMBO - Museo di Arte Moderna di Bologna - Via Don Minzoni 14 - Telefono: 051 6496611
Museo del Grigioverde - Via G. Dozza, 24 - Tel.:051 461100
Museo del Patrimonio Industriale - Via Beverara, 123 - Tel.:051 6356611
Museo del Risorgimento - c/o Casa Carducci - P.zza Carducci, 5 - Tel.:051 347592
Museo del Soldatino - c/o Villa Mazzacorati - Via Toscana, 19 - Tel.:051 6149574
Museo dell' Assistenza Infermieristica - Via di Barbiano, 1/10 - Tel.: 051 6366657
Museo della Comunicazione "Mille voci ...mille suoni" - Via Col di Lana, 7/n - Tel.: 051 6491008
Museo della Resistenza - Via Sant'Isaia, 20 - Tel.: 051 3397220
Museo della Sanità di Bologna - Via Clavature, 8 - Tel.:051 230260
Museo dell'Istituto Nazionale di Apicoltura - Via Saliceto, 80 - Tel.: 051 353103
Museo Ducati - Via Cavalieri Ducati, 3 - Tel.:051 6413343
Museo Ebraico - Via Valdonica, 1/5 - Tel.:051 2911280
Museo per la memoria di Ustica - c/o Ex Magazzino ATC - Via di Saliceto, 5 - Tel.: 051 6496611
Museo Tattile di Pittura Antica e Moderna - Via Castiglione, 71 - Tel.: 051 332090
Raccolta Lercaro - Via Riva di Reno, 57 - Tel.:051 2961159
Urban Center di Bologna Sottopasso via Rizzoli, - entrata in piazza Re Enzo - Tel.:051 271006

Musei Ecclesiastici* / *Church Museums* / *los museos eclesiásticos

Museo della Beata Vergine di San Luca - piazza di Porta Saragozza, 2/a - Tel.: 051 6447421
Museo di San Domenicoc/o Chiesa di San Domenico - Piazza S. Domenico, 13 - Tel.: 051 6400411
Museo di Santo Stefano c/o Chiesa Santo Stefano - Via S. Stefano, 24 - Tel.: 051 223256

Catholic masses in foreign languages

For the **Philipino** community - Convento delle Suore dei Poveri, at 11.15 a.m - **every Sunday.**
"El Shadday" charismatic community,chiesa del SS. Salvatore, via Volto Santo 1; at

3.00 p.m. - **every Sunday.**

Mass in **Tagalog** - *Contact*: Fr. Giuseppe Benassi,Basilica di S. Maria dei Servi, Strada Maggiore 43.

For the **Nigerian** community - Parrocchia del Cuore Immacolato di Maria,via Mameli 5, Borgo Panigale; at 4.00 p.m. **every 2nd and 3rd Sunday** of the month.

Misa en **espanol** - Oratorio San Donato, via Zamboni 5 **- Cada dominco** a la hora 17.00.

Mass in **singalee** - Chiesa del Baraccano, via Baraccano – at 12.00 noon - **every 2nd Sunday** of the month.

Msza swieta **po polsku -** Santa Caterina di Strada Maggiore, 56ks. Wlodzimierz Dziduch SChr (tel. 3466896377) O godz. 15.30.w kazda niedziele.

Messe en **arabe -** *Contactez*: don Davide Righi, Seminario Arcivescovile, piazzale Bacchelli 4.

Mass in **indonesian -** *Contact*: Fr. Jean-Paul, Basilica di San Francesco, piazza Malpighi 9.

Messa per **eritrei** e **rumeni** *Rivolgersi a* don Alberto Gritti, tel. 051/262426

CHURCHES OF OTHER CONFESSIONS

Synagogue – Via dei Gombruti, 9, tel. 051.23.20.66; **Seventh-day Adventist Christian Church** – Via delle Lame, 83, Tel. 051.55.56.09; **Evangelical Methodist Church -** 051 23.92.27

CLIMATE

It is continental since it is not influenced by sea.

Winter can even be very severe and snowfalls are not infrequent.

Summer is warm and especially sweltering due to high air humidity; the warmest months are July and August, during which temperature can even reach 37°.

Mid seasons usually are mild, rainy and brief. Often spring switches to summer ever since the first days of May, and also the Winter can already appear in certain days at the end of October.

Windy days are few, and this contributes to fog and haze formation, as well as air pollution persistence as a consequence of both the transit and local traffic, and the emissions of combustion products from heating systems and industrial plants.

GLOSSARY

Apse: it is an architectural element having the shape of a truncated vault. The top of the apse is called *"apse conch"*, and generally has a semi-dome shape.

Aquamanile: The aquamanile was a vessel with spout and handle that was accompanied by a basin. It was used to wash the hands while eating at the table from ancient times until the end of the 17th century.

Altarpiece: painted or sculptured tablet located on the altar as a decoration.

Pointed arch: The pointed arch is a two-centre arch that includes arcades belonging to circumferences having a radius longer or equal to the base of the arch itself. It is typical of Gothic architecture.

Ogival arch: The **vaulting rib** (also called **ogive**) is an *architectural element* typical of Roman and Gothic architectures. It forms the structure of a vault or a dome and divides its surface, thus directing the thrusts to the supporting pillars.

Flying buttress: it is an asymmetrical *architectural element* used to restrain and discharge to the ground the side forces, as well as the forces towards the outside of the building top. For this purpose, the impost levels on each pier are located at distinct heights, often with such a remarkable difference that it sometimes resembles a half-arch.

Sandstone: it is a sedimentary origin *rock* consisting of sand-sized grains.

BIANCONI Carlo: he was an Italian *painter* that worked between the 18th and the 19th centuries.

CARRACCI Ludovico: he was an Italian *painter* that worked between the 16th and the 17th centuries.

Cenoby: community of monks living in a monastery and obeying the same rule.

Coping: it is a curve and projecting *moulding* being concave or cyma-shaped.

Buttress: it is a support with quadrangular section placed in certain spots of the building walls and used as a reinforcement and counterforce.

Spire: it is an *architectural element* typical of Gothic art. It is often a synonym of steeple or pinnacle.

Ambulatory: The **ambulatory** is a corridor running around the chorus and the apse, and denotes a characteristic feature of sacred Gothic architecture. This term derives from the Latin word *deambulare*, which means *"to walk"*.

DA IMOLA Innocenzo: he was an Italian painter of the 16th century. Innocenzo da Imola deserved the pseudonym "Rafael from Romagna" thanks to his classically harmonious style.

De CAROLIS Adolfo: he was an Italian *painter*, *illustrator*, *scholar*, *xylographer* and *photographer*, who worked between the end of the 19th century and the beginning of the 20th century.

DE CROCEFISSI Simone: he was an Italian *painter* of the 14th century.

DI GAIO Donato da Cernobbio: he was an Italian *architect* of the 16th century.

DI PAOLO Jacopo: he was an Italian *painter* that worked between the 14th and the 15th centuries.

FIORAVANTI Aristotele: he was an architect and engineer of the Renaissance period, who worked from the middle of the 15th century onwards.

GALLI BIBBIENA Francesco Maria: he was a *decorator* that worked between the 17th and the 18th centuries.

GANDOLFI Ubaldo: he was an Italian *painter* of the 18th century, who worked especially in Emilia.

GUERCINO: (Giovanni Francesco Barbieri, called il Guercino) he was an Italian *painter* of the 17th century.

Steeple: it is a high and thin decorative *architectural element*, which has a conical or pyramidal shape and is used as an ornament in the roofs of churches, belfries, towers, etc.

LOMBARDI Alfonso: he was an Italian *sculptor* of the 16th century that worked especially in Bologna where, although he lived a relatively short life, he executed many works, most of which are still housed in the most important churches in the city. He mainly executed *stucco-* and *terracotta* works, however he proved to be able to *sculpt marble* and to create *bronze panels*.

MARCHESI Giuseppe: he was a *painter* of the 18th century.

Frontal: (in Italian is *paliotto*, which derives from Latin word *palium*, "veil") it is the covering of the altar table front. It can be made of cloth or ivory, or it may be mosaic or worked with precious metals, such as silver.

PASSAROTTI Bartolomeo: he was an Italian *painter* of the 16th century.

PEDRINI Filippo: he was an Italian *painter* that worked between the 18th and the 19th centuries.

PERUZZI Baldassarre: (Baldassarre Tommaso Peruzzi) he was an Italian *painter* and *architect* of the 16th century specialized in building fortifications. He often co-operated with the most important artists of Italian Renaissance period, but usually he was more successful as an architect.

Pier: vertical support on which the vault is laid.

Pinnacle: it is a vertical *architectural element* typical of Gothic architecture.

Presbytery: it derives from "presbyter", and is a liturgical and architectural word used to denote that section of the church that surrounds the main altar and is reserved to the officiating clergy.

Prothyrum: it is an architectural word that derives from Greek and denotes a spire-shaped small portico. It is placed so as to protect and cover the main entrance of a church.

Quadreria: this word can denote a place where many paintings are housed or even the collection itself.

RENI Guido: he was one of the most important Italian *painters* of the 17th century.

Offset: it is a setback of the external or internal surface of the walls (so that the portion of wall above is less thick than the corresponding one below). Often it is used to create a resting surface for beams (that usually were made of wood).

ROSSETTI Biagio: he was an Italian *architect* and *urbanist* that worked between the 15th and the 16th centuries. He worked almost always at the court of Este in Ferrara, and designed and installed the construction of the famous *"Herculean addiction"*, that was commissioned to him by Duke Hercules I of Este in 1492. Thanks to this work he can be considered as the *first urbanist* who employed modern operating methods.

Tabernacle: In modern languages "tabernacle" usually denotes a box-shaped structure present in all churches of Catholic and other Christian confessions, in which the hosts consecrated after the Celebration of Eucharist are kept.

Telamon: it is a in-the-round or relief male *sculpture* used as a structural or decorative support, and often placed instead of columns or pilasters.

In-the-round technique: it is a sculpture technique consisting of sculpting the subject without being limited by the background. This technique allows the subject to be developed in 3 dimensions, so that the beholder can observe the subject from whatever point of view he wants to.

VENEZIANO Paolo: he is considered as the forerunner of the *painting in Veneto*, the origins of which date back to the 4th century.

ZANOTTI Davide: he was an Italian *painter* that worked in Bologna in the 18th century and at the beginning of the 19th century.

INDEX OF PLACES

TRAVEL NOTES